£500 a Week
from
Car Boot Sales

by
Roger Morgan

IMPERIA BOOKS LIMITED

First published 1993
by Imperia Books Ltd.
© 1993 Roger Morgan.

The 'characters' quoted in this book are composites, built up
out of the author's experience in the trade. No resemblance
to actual persons, is intended and any supposed resemblance
is entirely coincidental.

British Library Cataloguing
in Publication Data.
A catalogue record for this book
is available from the British Library.
ISBN 1 897656 03 3

Cover by Sarah Davies
Cover cartoon by Guy Parker-Rees
Typeset by Carter Wordsmiths, London

Published by
IMPERIA BOOKS LIMITED
Canada House, Blackburn Road, London NW6 1RZ

Printed in Great Britain by Black Bear Press Ltd., Cambridge

Contents

Introduction

Right, so you've paid your money and have this book in your hands, fingers quivering with impatience to know just how the hell you make £500 a week from what you thought was a 'two-bob' business or even a hobby.

Booting Language

Before we get started I'll explain, for the uninitiated, that 'two-bob' expression. This book is going to take you right inside the 'boot' business. If you are to understand the strange world of general dealing – and that's what car booting is – you'll need to know the language, the slang words and phrases that the folk in the 'biz' use to keep the 'civilians' (non dealers) and 'punters' (customers) in the dark about what goes on.

'Two-bob' means small-time, of no account financially or socially. A two-bob booter is the lowest order of animal in dealing, O.K.?

I've put this bit in so that you understand that when a strange word appears with something in brackets ( ) after it, I'm explaining the lingo. So by the time you get to the end of the book, you should be able to understand a dealing conversation without the need for an interpreter. If you get lost at any stage, refer to the Glossary at the back of the book.

Studying the Rules

I suggest that you read the book more than once before you dash out to make your first 'Monkey' (£500). There's a massive amount of knowledge in these pages and you won't make big money if you don't study the rules before starting to play the game.

Layout of the Book

The book is not laid out in strict sections for good reasons. Some subjects come under more than one heading and certain situations are linked to others in different chapters.

I'd like you to learn the game the way I did – not by a set of instructions but by experiencing the many and various sides of the trade until you grasp an over-all picture in your mind of what it is to be a dealer or professional booter and how the tricks of the trade work.

The Secret World of Booting

I've tried to make this book the most comprehensive work written so far on a trade that has always jealously guarded its secrets. Some are shocking, others amusing. But I doubt if there is anyone who reads it who won't find something that they didn't know before.

So, take my hand and I'll lead you, quite safely, through a world where blokes who can't even read or write properly often earn £1,000 in a day. Where ladies, who look anything from a bag of rags to a princess, earn more in a month than many folk earn in a year. Impossible? Ridiculous? Well my luvs, it's going on around you all the time and car boot sales are one of the places where the general public can see it and not even suspect it's happening!

Some Statistics

Economists and other gas bags, who've never done a real day's work in their lives, estimate that Britain's 'black economy' turns over 4 billion pounds a year. That's four thousand million pounds that never show up on paper; and car boot sales account for a large percentage of it. Sounds incredible doesn't it? But let's look at some facts and figures.

Every week-end, at least one million people visit or indulge in car booting. That's twice the number that attend league football matches, our national sport! Booting is fast becoming the most popular pastime in Great Britain. There will be at least one boot sale held each week-end in smaller towns or even in villages. Around the provinces, each of the larger towns may have two or three. Within a radius of 20 miles around a county town, you could find a dozen or more. Check your local paper for proof and then multiply that by the number of local papers.

On any Sunday, there are probably more than a thousand sales being held. Some sales will have 200 or more stalls, others as few as 20, so let's assume an average of a modest 50 – that's 50,000 stalls. If each stall takes an average of just £50 that's 2.5 million pounds. Multiply by 50 weeks and you have a turnover of 125 million pounds per year – and that is an UNDERESTIMATE.

How Much Do Booters Earn?

Fact is, on a reasonable day your average semi-pro booter takes well over £100 and pros take £250 to £300. 'But that's not £500' you say. I'm glad you noticed. It shows you're not completely stupid. BUT, the pro booter doesn't come out just on Sunday. There's Saturday sales, bank holidays, evening sales in summer, the 'good' stuff they send to auction rooms, big or specialized items sold through the 'free sheet' papers, deals done with other booters or dealers in the trade.

And you thought it was just a few quid on the side? Don't make me laugh. It's a big money biz with an annual turnover of more than a BILLION POUNDS. But you've got to know how it works if you want some of it. THAT'S WHAT THIS BOOK'S ALL ABOUT. Not about being two-bob, but about the big money and how to earn it.

Booting Is Popular

Why is booting so successful? There are a number of reasons. Street or open-air markets have always been popular for their combination of fairground and holiday atmosphere. They're more entertaining than conventional shops. It's like combining the pleasures of a walk with those of shopping, with the added attraction of low prices.

Car boot sales increase the promise of a bargain. It's a day out with no charge for admission or entertainment, and a chance to indulge that unique British passion for nosing into what other people have or had, and being able to buy it for less than they did. A sort of salve for jealousy if you like.

There is no doubt that the current economic situation, as politicians call it, or slump if you are honest, feeds the cheap goods market. As shop turnovers fall, boot sales rise. Can't afford new? Go to a boot sale! Everything you ever wanted is there at a tenth of the price. Once a punter gets hooked on boot gear, his or her patronage of shops reduces still further. Got to be a bit careful here or the Government might decide it's us wrecking the economy rather than them. Oh yes, we owe a lot to Mrs. T. She created a market for us that won't go away even if things do get better.

Boot punters are surprisingly loyal and many booters have their regular customers who phone up out of hours with requests for particular items. The booter, with a wide range of contacts is Mr. or Mrs. Fixit. A service industry combined with retailing AND ecology! TOP OF THE POPS so to speak. How green was my fiver?

Paid Fun

You must excuse these little jokes. Booters are a happy crowd and love a laugh. They enjoy what they do. It's a totally absorbing business. You learn all the time, make lots of friends, get paid very well, work when you like and never fear redundancy or the sack. Utopia really, if you don't mind actually working. Most consider it paid fun.

Come On In

Would you like a job like this? It's yours for the taking. And even if a million more people joined in, we couldn't over-supply the market nor run out of stock. Booters and dealers are still only recirculating ONE percent of the saleable stuff that goes to waste every year! There is an increasing demand for boot-type gear from the punters. The crowds get bigger every week.

Just as I was finishing this book, a vast new venue opened a few miles away from my home. The man organising it has invested a MILLION POUNDS in it and its main income is from boot sales. On the first Sunday of trading 10,000 people turned up to buy and the roads for miles around were jammed with traffic trying to get to the venue. This is the boom industry of the bankrupt Nineties and will boom on into the next century. COME ON IN, IT'S LOVELY!

Chapter 1
In the Beginning

The Oldest Trade

Dealing is as old as the first goods made. I won't say it's the oldest profession for that would give you the wrong idea. But it is one of the oldest trades.

As soon as man began to make things, some bright spark saw a way of making a living without the work of producing the goods himself. That's what dealing is – transferring the things someone wants money for to someone who will pay money for them, and in so doing make a profit, known in the trade as the 'mark-up'.

If you make goods and sell them you are not a dealer but a manufacturer. If you buy a manufacturer's goods and sell them on to a retailer you are a wholesaler. If you buy from a wholesaler or manufacturer and sell to the user, you are a retailer. BUT if you buy stuff that's been through the trade before, new or second hand you are a DEALER, whether you sell to trade or public. It is IMPORTANT that you understand the difference. Until you do you're not a dealer. A dealer buys from many different sources and has many outlets for his goods. He or she is a general factotum in trade and an important part of the economy.

The merchants of the Middle Ages established many of the trade practices that still exist today. They caused money to come into regular use in Europe. Before then, most small-time trade was by barter – the exchange of goods without money. The merchants, many of whom had a dealing side to their trade, needed more flexibility and coins gave just that. Later, they were instrumental in bringing paper money into common use.

Buying and Selling

There is an old adage in sales that says 'Nothing happens until someone sells something'. This is absolutely true. Nothing will happen in your biz until you sell something and obtain the cash to buy something else to sell. Or get something and sell it. Without sales the world grinds to a halt.

Those who buy and sell are vital to the economy. They are the life blood of industry and providers to the consumer.

Dealing is an honourable and respectable trade. More folk have become millionaires by buying and selling than by any other method. You could do the same and you don't need money to start!

M & S

A man set up a little table in a North of England market and sold a few pennyworth of ribbon and thread. He started with nothing more than that in an economic climate far harder than today's. That business is known today as Marks & Spencer. If you haven't heard of them then you're possibly a Mongolian shepherd or an alien being. Either of them could do a car boot sale if they follow the advice in this book – even if it had to be read out to them. In fact the Mongolian shepherd would probably do better than some booters I've seen who are stuck for an answer if you say 'hello' and even THEY make money.

Car Booting

What's so special about car booting? A very great deal. It's one of the few areas of business where you can start with nothing at all and make cash money IMMEDIATELY. And worthwhile money at that. If you've been scratching around in commission only or part-time work for peanuts, or perhaps delivering papers or pushing leaflets through doors, you'll break down in tears when I tell you that the average booter earns about £20 an hour for his efforts, with virtually zero overheads. Many make far more.

Its Origins

Where did it come from, this phenomenon that makes money from nothing? Where else but that font of all that is commercial, the U.S.A. In America, a classless society they say, money and what it can purchase is the measure of who you are.

The post world war boom in the States led to ever-increasing production of consumer goods. The power of media advertising, particularly in television, and the rise in disposable incomes and easy credit, gave average Americans the ability to stuff their homes with every conceivable appliance and gimmick available. As the novelty of the new toys wore off, garages became crammed with redundant items constantly being replaced with the latest model in everything from household to sports goods. Americans were becoming buried under a mountain of obsolete goods.

It became a national joke. A popular radio and later television comedy show in the late 1940s to early 1950s, called Life of Riley, regularly featured a scene where the long-suffering family man, Riley, opened the hall closet to be immediately deluged by the redundant goods crammed in there. Americans loved the show because they could identify with the scenes of suburban family life. It mirrored their own predicament of acquisitiveness gone crazy.

Garage Sales

Then came the catalyst. Someone, no one knows who, came up with a bright idea. Why not hold a sale in your own garage and clear out all the unwanted stuff? That way, you turned redundant goods into cash that could be used to buy even more fun stuff! The GARAGE SALE was born.

Trunk Sales

It was only a short step from there for commercially minded Americans to see that if you could take the goods to a wider public, even more could be sold. Using giant estate cars and pick-up trucks, they would gather in a local field or at a 'market' (supermarket) parking lot to sell or exchange their unwanted goods. The idea caught on like wildfire and soon a name was coined for it – TRUNK SALES, 'trunk' being American for the English 'boot'.

In Britain

In Britain, the consumer boom didn't get under way until the mid fifties, but the increase in mail order and hire-purchase as a way of obtaining goods on credit got things moving.

'You've never had it so good' said the then Prime Minister, Harold Macmillan in 1959. The credit card appeared a few years later and Britain was confirmed as a consumer society along American lines. Garages began to fill up and 'built in obsolescence' became a manufacturing buzz phrase.

Britain largely skipped the garage sale thing and the first car boot sales appeared in the early seventies. The 'stock' from the consumer boom had matured nicely and was ready to be re-cycled.

Boot Sales

It was a slow start at first. But as the effects of the first recession since the war were felt in 72-73, the boot sale began to catch on. By 1979 it was an established idea. There were new and nasty developments about. Massive redundancies caused an army of unemployed to grow. Mention of the 'black economy' became common in political speeches.

New ideas started to take hold. Ecology and 'green' viewpoints began to appear in the media. The idea of re-cycling goods came out of the 'Steptoe' rag and bone and junk-shop sphere. It became everybody's business.

There had been junk markets for hundreds of years. In the immediate post war period of severe shortage they had a place, which faded with the growth of consumerism. Agricultural areas had their 'dead stock' markets – traditional auctions where poorly paid country folk, still very backward by city standards, could exchange old goods cheaply and keep going. Auction houses handled better quality unwanted goods and the antique trade's requirements.

But the boot sale was different. It was a whole new concept. A camp follower that picked up the wreckage of the consumer boom and turned junk into money with no 'middle man' apparent. Let's listen to Richard, one of the pioneers of booting in the early seventies.

Richard's Story

The Good Life

I first got interested in booting after reading about 'Auto-jumbles' in an American car magazine. Car enthusiasts gathered to swap and sell spare parts at 'meets' where prices were low and the whole thing was a bit of a day out for car freaks. The mag mentioned that similar things were happening among surf and sports enthusiasts in California, swapping and selling the expensive 'toys' of their hobbies to get stuff that was too dear to buy new in shops

I suppose it was a sort of extension of the hippie culture, where you could have the benefits of the good life without working yourself to death to afford them.

First Deals

I had been messing about in the buying and selling lark for a while – getting stuff here and there and selling to dealers who made big profits from the goods they bought from me for a few quid. After a while I managed to get a stall at one of the big London markets selling general stuff. But I got the feeling that there was a much wider market than the regular crowd that turned up there.

Sites

Encouraged by what I read in the Yank mag, I sounded out a few mates about setting up a one-off sale on a cleared site near where I lived in South East London. I figured that I had nothing to lose bar a day's work at the market; and Sunday seemed like a day when absolutely nothing happened on my 'manor' (home area), so why not give it a go?

To cut a long story short, the result wasn't bad and we kept going till the bloke that owned the site put the block on it. By then we'd been going for about six weeks and the half dozen car boots had grown to about twenty. I looked around for a new site and met a bloke who reckoned that a site further out toward the sticks would work. He knew just the place and the bloke that owned it. We were in business again.

This time I really went for it. I advertised it as a place where anyone could sell their own gear – I never gave a thought to charging for pitches. On that first Sunday, thirty faces turned up to sell gear from their car boots. This was IT. I got a free pitch to sell my own gear and a crowd, drawn in by the novelty, who paid more for stuff than I would get at the old market stall.

Everything was great till the bloke who owned the site came to me and asked for his cut of the action. This just hadn't occurred to me, honest. I went round the other faces and a quick whip round had everybody happy again. That little venue kept going for over a year till the local council got ratty and stopped it under Sunday Trading laws, but nothing was going to stop me now.

Licence to Print Money

Again, to cut a long story short, I found a new site, charged pitch rental at a couple of quid a go but still kept my own little stall going. Within eighteen months I had a real business under way. I had to give up my own stall to organise sales. As soon as I put an ad for a venue in the paper, the phone never stopped ringing. It was a licence to print money as they say.

The Good Times

That was near seventeen years ago. By 1988, my brother and father had joined me and we were organising sales, full trader markets, sports and charity events, anything with an outdoor flavour. I also own a lot of property, land and other types of business.

Although times are said to be hard, my business is diverse enough to survive without problems. If I had to raise cash quickly, I would still think of boot sales as an immediate source of cash money. There is no quicker way other than borrowing dough – and that's a mugs' game AND you have to pay it back!

––––––

So, there's the story of one young man who became a millionaire from nothing by the instant cash character of booting.

Richard's is not an isolated success. There are lots like him who started in the same way. Some are still in the game. Others took their profits and funded other businesses. But the same thing is repeated in every story – the fast cash nature of the business and the way it makes money from almost nothing.

Next, let's talk to Eric who's been booting for about ten years and is still a stall holder.

Eric's Story

Made Redundant

I got into booting when I was made redundant from a chemical processing firm in 1980. I had a mortgage and a family and was scared stiff when my job folded. I almost went potty trying to find work. I got so depressed with debts and trying to make ends meet that if it hadn't been for my wife and kiddies I think I would have done myself in.

I'd been on the dole for close to a year and was wandering round a boot sale, looking for cheap bits to try to make something of Christmas, when I saw one of the sellers doing a deal – buying some stuff from a chap.

It Hit Me!

I thought of selling some bits we had left at home. Then I noticed that the man behind the stall was paying for the stuff he'd bought off a roll of notes that must have contained hundreds of pounds. I'd never pinched anything in my life, but at that moment I was tempted. Then it hit me. Why couldn't I do what he was doing?

I asked around and it seemed that you just drive on to the site and sell your stuff. Next week I was there, I made about £50 for the bits I sold, and it cost me £3 to set up and do it.

I never looked back. I will admit that I kept signing the dole for three months and that was wrong. But the minute I could see that things were going to work out, I signed off and it was the greatest feeling in the world.

It took time to learn the tricks of the trade – but it's not difficult, just common sense and a bit of chat really. I've made mistakes of course but I never lost much – just didn't make as much as I should have done.

My Life Now

We're in a new house now. A bigger one in a better area. The money I earned at the Works seems a joke against what I make now. We take nice holidays and money's not a problem.

All right, I work hard and, I suppose, to the neighbours I've got a bit of a 'totter' image. But there's a brand new car on the drive, paid for, as well as my working motor. My kids have all the bikes and stuff that's important to them and the wife's happy cos we've got no worries.

I don't want to get any bigger than this. It suits me. Some booters turn over fortunes. Well good luck to them, that's their business. If there's something special we need, I can always do a bit more to get it.

I pay cash for everything and if dealing's taught me one thing it's that there's always a cheaper price. I laugh at High Street shop prices. Through contacts I can get most things at less than cost. Our food comes from the shops, but everything else comes through 'the trade'. That's another perk of dealing.

Working Straight

I work 'straight' as they say. I have an accountant who tidies up the simple books I do and makes sure I don't pay more tax than necessary.

The benefits of having your own business are incredible. To live our kind of life style working for someone else, I would have to earn about a thousand a week before tax. It sounds funny I know, but the bloke who made me redundant did me a favour. I would never work for someone else again.

––––––

Above are just two true stories of successful booters. They show it's a business that can be as big or small as you want.

Some booters operate in addition to an existing job but that makes it hard work and a seven day week. The majority who start like this either move into full-time dealing or disappear from the scene because it didn't suit them or they just couldn't put in the effort required. Like any other thing, if you want success you have to work for it – but not as hard as most employed folk.

There are those to whom it is just a hobby that pays. They're the small fish who enjoy the fun, friendship and atmosphere of booting. They can be as young as 12 or 13 years and turn up with a suitcase of stuff – or over 80 and still trading from an old Morris estate that looks as rickety as they do. But the old 'uns are often still sharp as razors when it comes to a deal and I've watched kids grow up into big time dealers and venue organizers. It's a biz where any number can win.

Go For It

So, let's go for it. Let's get to where the aroma of hot dogs, burgers and chips mixes with the smell of junk and money – where the sound of a hundred car stereos competes with cries of 'you'll never buy cheaper' – where the 'saucer-eyed' punters crush on to the 'ven' (site) to make us rich as they seek out the bargains. Let's go booting!

Chapter 2
The Basics

Booting is a game where you can start from scratch. You need nothing more than a car and a little stock.

The Vehicle

Anything will do. I wouldn't recommend an Austin Healey Sprite but I have seen booters selling from a sports model more than once! The ideal motor is a hatch back or estate.

The classic dealer vehicle is the Volvo estate car – the 245 as it's called. This motor is just about perfect. It has an incredible van-sized payload area and easy access to the rear low-loading tail with no obstructions. It's made for the trade. And there's more! Fit a tow hitch and a safari type roof-rack – that's the sort that goes from the top of the rear hatch right forward to over the bonnet – and you can easily transport 2.5 TONS of stuff to the target.

I've known blokes who carried three or even four tons like this and then wondered why this wonderful car let them down after several years of that kind of abuse, not realizing that the motor had paid for itself many times over.

O.K., so you can't afford a Volvo, even at trade price (we'll come to how that's done later). Even a Fiesta hatch will carry enough of the right stuff to earn you more than you'll ever get working on the check-out at Tesco – in a week! An ordinary saloon car can also do that at the right sale.

I tend to avoid vans. If this is all you've got, well use it. But vans say 'trade', which makes the punter wary. Also, and it's a generalisation I know, but van sellers offer more 'dogs' (dud electrics etc.) than car sellers. There are fewer vans than cars being used – so naturally the punters are nervous of van-sold stuff.

The public may be stupid, in the main, but people do wise up to the obvious trends. It's like this. Scruffy van + scruffy seller = dodgy stock. So they keep on walking or try to buy very cheap. Ipso facto, van man makes less dough.

Use a brand new van and it's little better. Now you're an obvious TRADER, particularly if you have a custom-made 'flash' (that's the term for those tubular steel stalls that come to pieces).

Joe Public, in his quaint way, likes to think that he's dealing with an amateur, not with a pro trader unless he's selling new goods – but that's not booting, is it? Booting is secondhand stuff. Yes, even when it's antique. After all what is an antique but OLD secondhand stuff? Don't let words fool you. But more on the 'Ant' trade later.

Your Stall

You don't even need a stall, but it is handy to present stuff closer to the buyer, also to keep it off wet grass in a field situation. Lots of sellers just spread out a blanket or old curtain to display the goods. This works quite well, particularly with small 'pot' (china) items. In the biz, everything in china or what have you – stuff that smashes when you drop it – is pot or glass. The fancy terms and maker names are just for the punter.

One chap I know, does very well from quite ordinary pot and glass. He spreads it out on two very large, Italian, crimson silk curtains and hey presto! The ordinary stuff looks worth far more. The goods are improved by their environment, see? Display is important. Five saucepans on a rack will do better than five in a box or on the ground.

A television on a stand fetches more than one sitting on a box. Why do you think shops spend so much on their window displays? Because the better-displayed item fetches more and sells faster.

Ten good items of clothing on a rack will make far more dough than a hundred in a heap, fronted by a bit of card saying 'All Clothes 20p'.

Moral? Don't pile it high and sell it cheap – that's for supermarkets on 1% profit. We're looking for 1,000%, or MORE. I'd rather sell one good coat for a 'tenner' than give change to fifty 20p punters. While I'm wasting time like that, I'm losing money.

Really, it's best to stay away from the 'stinking old clothes' line. That's for the losers and 'minnows'. If you come by a 'job' (a big lot sold cheap) load of clothing, weed out any good, single items and sell the rest for a fiver or so to one of the two-bob booters. Let them waste time. A pound for a black sack full is about market price.

Stalling Out (Setting up the Stall)

All I've ever used is two wallpaper pasting tables.

Here's how I set up my 'gaff' (selling area). The two tables, end to end, give me twelve feet of 'flash' (frontage area). I stand behind them with the motor, hatch open, end-on behind me.

In front of the tables go 'the boxes'. These are small items of low value divided into types – electrical, domestic, tools and D.I.Y., toys, miscellaneous. Each box has a 'bin price', i.e. 'all at 50p each' or £1 etc.

Next in line, books, in two large strong suitcases. Why? Cos you don't want to unpack or re-pack books. They're out of the motor, lid open and selling. If it rains – lid closed and stock protected. The two cases are

1 Modern paperbacks/hardbacks.
2 Old or collectable.

More detail on books in the antiques chapter.

Next on the 'front line' (in front of the stall), vacuum cleaners. Always a seller, but must be where they can be examined without causing disruption to the flash. Put them on a bit of carpet – that seems to help the sale. Even then, some idiot will ask 'Is that a cleaner, mate?' You'll get used to it. It's a good job that there are people like that or people like us wouldn't make money. After all, with his brains he'll never have the dough to buy new, will he?

At the far end come the 'sauces' (saucepans) and fryers. And on the table above, other small kitchenware.

Keep the stuff in strict groups. A saucepan buyer may want other 'kitch' (kitchen) stuff – so make it easy to find. Don't go jumbling it all up. It's confusing and looks bad.

Your gaff says a lot about the kind of seller you are. Respectable stall = respectable seller. Trust is established and sales result.

Your Appearance

While we're about it, let's look at personal image. Many folk buy the seller, not the goods. It's the old salesman's adage, first sell yourself. Even if you're selling junk, don't look junk. Booting is a hard job and wears out clothes, but always look smart.

Lads, shave please, unless you sport a beard. Your personal style is your own business, of course, but I wear good quality country tweeds with a cap and wax jacket if necessary. I don't like wearing a collar and tie but do sometimes, or a cravat or polo-neck sweater. You don't have to dress up. You can wear jeans and a tee shirt, set out next to me and wonder why I took more money.

Old images die hard. The public still trust traditional styles and traditional LIES. Why do you think politicians wear suits? To make people trust them! They're far bigger rogues than you or me.

Ladies

No, I've not forgotten you. The best lady booter I know, dresses like a duchess, sells absolute rubbish and makes a fortune. Muriel, that's her name, looks like she came straight from a beautician's at 6 a.m. Her style and elegance are breathtaking. The punters are like putty in her hands and she can get more for a bit of Taiwan fake 'cappo' (that's Cappo di Monte china) than shops get for the real thing. It's the way she sells 'em, see?

Muriel once took an awful, black plaster 'market shop' vase from me for a pound – which I thought was robbery. I watched in admiration as she unloaded it for £8.50 to a punter who thought he'd been done the biggest favour of his life. Study your image. Let the punter buy YOU first, and the goods will then sell automatically. But a good line in chat helps. More on that later.

Back to the Stall

Where were we? Oh yes, the stall.

On the table, next, is a black felt-covered board. This displays little antique bits, low value jewellery and curios. The expensive stuff, good watches etc., go in a lockable, glass-topped case right under your nose. Thieves are a constant problem.

Next come the radios, cassettes, car stereos and bits – all just under my watchful eye. Big stuff at the back, raised on small cardboard boxes, small bits at the front, but nothing too stealable.

Bigger stuff, small furniture, bulkier items, go on either side of the vehicle rear, on the ground or on the roof rack where they are well displayed.

Stuff can be hung from the side gutters of the motor to make best use of least space. If you're using a trailer let it double up as display area.

Waste nothing! Show further stock inside the vehicle. If you sell out, you didn't take enough stock – a crime, for you could have made more dough! Aim to come back with about 25% of what you took and NEVER, as some lazy swines do, pack up before the last punter has gone.

Dropping the Sheet (End of Day's Trading)

Some of the best deals I have done were when half the sellers were packing up. The disappointed look on the late arrival punter's face says it all and the seller who is still 'stalled out' in full glory has the field to himself. It's like a sale with one stall – yours!

Ask any shopkeeper if he would like the competition to close up and leave all the customers for him!

Never be like the bloke who once set up next to me. All day he complained about everything – the site, the punters, the difficulty in getting stock, the weather. All the time he was moaning to me, I had been taking a steady, modest rate of trade.

He was the first to start packing up and had had a lousy day, according to him. I was horrified when a punter asked the price of an item still out on his flash and he replied 'I'm closed, luv, you should have got here earlier'. I said nothing but waited till the crestfallen woman drew level with me. I then engaged her in casual conversation and apologized for nextdoor's attitude. Now would that be beneath your dignity?

I was rewarded with £40 worth of trade from that lady, and my moaning neighbour stood and watched as I took her money – and he STILL thought it was all a matter of luck! If you think he was right, chuck this book away now and bother no further. But please don't ask for your money back, because if I gave you the Horn of Plenty you'd complain that it was too heavy to carry home.

Large Items

Talking of heavy things, here's a tip about what not to sell at a boot. Let's suppose that a chap offered you ten near-new washing machines for next to nothing. We're speaking hypothetically here, so don't start on about why were they so cheap.

Think about your market before you buy. A washer is a big, heavy, nasty thing to move. How many folk at a boot sale will have a way of getting it home? How many of those who have the transport, will want a washer, assuming we're not giving them away? No, things this size are 'home sale' deals. You buy them and advertise them in the local paper at a good profit.

In the vehicle, one washer takes up the space of say six portable T.V.s or ten video machines. Think how much more money ten, even tatty vids can make at £25 each, against one washer that you had to sell too cheap rather than take home – or perhaps dropped on your foot loading up, putting you out of the game for weeks maybe?

That's just common sense, you say. Well you'd be surprised at the number of washers I've 'stolen' (obtained at a give-away price) from booters who didn't want to take them home but couldn't get their price. O.K., I humped them home in the empty wagon after a good day. But I did sell them for a great profit through the free paper. A bit of thought is all it needs. You have to see the wider field if you go dealing.

So let's remember. Small and easy to lift is beautiful in our game. 1,000 watches sold at £1 each is better than a three-piece suite at £50!

But, says you, a while ago you said DON'T pile it high and sell it cheap. Right! I'm glad you're watching points.

Those 1,000 watches cost us £100 from a job dealer. They take up the space of an overnight bag. They sell at any sale, a few at a time and look good on the flash. You don't have to give change that often on a pound sale, so it's a good bread and butter line. O.K., so they're crap; but who complains when a £1 watch has a fit after 6 months? A £1,000 watch would have to last over 500 years to be better value. Now, are you starting to learn? Good!

Don't Start Yet

Possibly, by now you can't wait to get started but I would ask you, if you will, to read the whole book before you dash out and get disappointed. There's a great deal more I want you to understand that will prevent you selling yourself short and giving the unworthy public a treat. Fact is, you can sell anything at a boot sale, I've seen everything from a small railway train to a Viking helmet – and nothing surprises me. But WHERE to sell? That's important.

Venues

Now I could pack out the pages of this book with an enormous list of boot venues but I would be wasting my time and your money. I really do like to give value for money and a list of venues would not be such.

Why? Simple. First, if you live in say, Doncaster, venues in Devon won't be of much interest, will they? I could do a region by region list, but the vast majority of it would be of no use to you would it? Secondly, boot venues are a bit like mushrooms, they appear overnight and disappear just as quickly. So any list I might present, would be out of date and therefore bad value before you ever got it.

Sure, there are very big occasional venues that weather the storms of fate and seem indestructible but these are few and far between. The boot sale is a moving animal. I can look back three years and hardly any of the venues I used then are still going. They ended for quite legitimate reasons. Redevelopment of the land, new owners not in tune with sales, changes in roads, and so on.

On the other hand, in the last couple of months, several new venues, well attended by the public, have come into being and have replaced the old order. So, a list of venues would, I reckon, be a waste of good space when you paid money for information that will be of use, right?

Boot sale organisers want to be successful and make lots of dough. To achieve this they must attract stalls AND the public. They spend a lot of money advertising their venues in local papers, with posters, even with ads on local radio! Why should I waste your money telling you about venues, when organisers desperately want you to know about them for free? Any worth-while sale advertises. If it doesn't, don't go – cos the punters won't know it's on and they won't be there. Common sense?

Locating Good Venues and Pitches

Now for the clever stuff. There's an old military adage that says 'Time spent on reconnaissance is seldom wasted'.

I NEVER use a new venue before I have visited it as a customer. This way you put yourself right before you sell. Venues can have 'dead corners' that flatten trade. You need to know the good spots AND the bad 'uns.

Are there toilets, if so where? Where do the food vendors set up? You might think that a pitch next to the hot dog van will be good – but at a busy sale, your flash could be permanently obscured by a long line of folk waiting to buy food. True they might be a captive audience, but how many punters missed your pitch behind the crowd? This is why you 'recce'.

Food sellers tend to be regulars at the 'ven'. Watch the food buyers and see which way they move off when they've got their grub. Your pitch wants to be about four gaffs down from the food in the direction that most eaters take.

If you watch carefully, you will see that the eaters will move off quite quickly as they get the grub, missing the stall next to it, and possibly the next one. They usually walk AWAY from the line of food customers, not back along it. By about the fourth gaff along they slow down and start looking as they eat. Four down from food on the 'clear' side is a DIAMOND of a pitch! Cos that's about where most stop and munch.

Never set up near toilets. Folk always move away from them quickly and usually approach even faster! Either way 'bog' pitches are a loser and every crying child on the site will pass your gaff. There is nothing like a child's cry to break the magic of your 'spiel'(sales talk) to the punter on the brink of buying that item you thought would never sell!

Your recce should also tell you average prices being asked for commonplace goods at that venue. What is and isn't shifting, what sort of sellers use the site, what kind of punters attend. What's the strength of the competition and what alternative attractions are present.

Bad Attractions

Avoid sites with lots of fairground stuff – bouncy castles, rides etc. They tend to attract a large percentage of non-buyers just out to gawp or entertain children.

The best punters have no children under 10 years with them. Don't concentrate on toys and only have them in stock if you can get them for nothing. Folk with small kids are usually hard-up. Better-off folk with children don't buy secondhand toys. So the poor folks' kids will play with your toy stock until they're dragged away by their skint parents and you've provided free entertainment – and made? NOTHING!

Toy stock should be the bigger, better stuff, priced so low that it's gone in the first hour. I repeat, NEVER BUY TOYS. I'll show you how to get them for nothing later on.

When you recce a venue, try to see it empty as well as trading. This way you know where you want to be, pitch wise, on a selling day. A site will look a lot different at 6 a.m. than when trading is in full swing. Look for things to avoid – muddy patches, uneven ground, long grass, overhanging trees. There's nothing like a tree dripping dew on stock, punter and you to damp-down trade.

Exceptions

There are exceptions, of course. In summer – when we get some – under the trees is a 'brahma' (that's even better than a 'diamond'). In really hot weather, a sheltered spot will draw in the punters. Outside trading, all day long in hot weather, is exhausting. I've seen sellers carted off to hospital with heat-stroke more than once. The effect of climate on your selling technique can be devastating and punters suffer too. So the shaded pitch is an oasis.

I have a favourite venue at a big hospital site where, when the old thermom climbs, I will be found 'under the tree, four down from the ice-cream lady'. I pay the promoter a bit extra to reserve this prime pitch and do a fab trade in 'shades' (sun glasses), sun oil, and cologne (bought in winter at rock bottom), apart from my other stock. There's always a crowd round my gaff. And do you know, other booters STILL don't understand why I make so much money!

Seasonal Earners

The smart booter takes advantage of the seasons. In the depth of winter you can buy nicely packaged, cheap sun-oil at £5 per crate of 100 bottles. Job dealers or wholesalers specialising in market trader goods have plenty of 'sunny' (sun-oil) at giveaway prices in winter. They look like expensive stuff that sells for a fiver in the shops and, when the old 'currant bun' (sun) is doing the biz, they 'walk away' (sell very quickly) at £1.50 each. That's THREE THOUSAND per cent mark up! You find a safe investment that will earn this kind of dough and the world will fight its way to your door.

Stock for your First Sale

So, we've covered starting up, what to sell and where, but you've still not got stock to do your first sale, have you?

Most booters started off by clearing out all the junk from their own home and were so amazed by what they got for it they just kept going.

But there comes a point where you run out of the stuff you bought and never needed in the first place. This is the moment of truth in booting that sorts out the dabblers from real dealers.

It's not a bad idea to have a clear-out at home, because if you are 'going pro' you'll need all the space you can get. My own house is like a cross between a warehouse and a junk yard. Dealing is a way of life, not just a trade, and it can take over. But more about dealing in the next chapter, where we will find the sources of that, supposedly, hard-to-find stock.

Chapter 3
The Stuff and How to Get It

Stock! The life blood of our trade. Without it you can't do business. This chapter will surprise or even shock people who thought they were dealers. Half the tricks of the trade are in how you obtain stock and there are some very strange ways and means in dealing. Not all of them are strictly honest and some are downright criminal. I don't advocate crime as a way of life – that would be unethical. But if you are going to be a pro booter/dealer, you will need to KNOW exactly what goes on – the good and the bad.

First Steps

Let's start right at the beginning. The next step for the booter who's sold all his own unwanted stuff, is to tout around family and friends for stock. Unless you have a very large or very tolerant family, this source will soon dry up.

You'll find yourself less and less welcome on social visits, which inevitably turn into looting raids as your lust for easy money overcomes any family feeling you might have displayed before you became a dealer. As the bug bites, every journey is a hunt. Every builder's skip, dustbin, relative's shed or garage, even their living room is fair game in your quest for further spoils. You become a 'boot pirate' (see chapter 5 for definition).

Having run out of family and friends, you look for fresh fields. You won't need to go on chasing the old lot anyway, cos they'll soon be round on the scrounge when word of your new-found affluence gets out.

Jumble Sales

The next move is usually jumble sales. You may think that these small, parochial fund-raising events are gentle affairs. WRONG!

Today, the 'jumbly' is total war with no Geneva Convention. A good booter can make fifty to one hundred pounds from a fiver's worth of jumbly stuff! But there's a real art to being a 'jumble raider' (a booter who specialises in getting good stock from jumbles).

I no longer do many jumblies myself, only the odd one here and there. So I will pass on the know-how of an acknowledged expert.

This is where we start to see what might be termed the unacceptable face of dealing, so let's be quite clear on an important point. I can in no way condone the illegal methods that some dealers use to obtain stock. There is a whole world of difference between being 'smart' and being a thief. But where, as in the next story, there is dishonesty and crime, I will not hide it. I promised to give you the unvarnished truth for it is important you know what you are up against.

I have seen 'Penguin' Pat in action many times and can vouch that he is the best jumble raider in the history of the game. He is a clever man – but this is spoiled by some of his unpleasant methods. Pat got the name 'Penguin' from his perfection of the 'penguin swipe', which he describes in his report from the jumble warfare front.

Pat Reaveals All

The Recce

The most important thing in jumble raiding is to get a preview of the sale. It's no good wasting an hour or more queueing up for a sale, only to find nothing worth having when you finally get in. You need to know if there are good 'steals' (things obtained for near nothing) to be had before you wait, or even get them before the queuers ever see them.

People think that a jumbly is just a load of old junk. They couldn't be more wrong. When decent folk, with no dealer knowledge, collect a lot of stuff to raise a bit of money for their organization or charity, the odds are that, unless there is a dealer among them – and that's unlikely – there are going to be things among the stuff worth far more than they hope to raise from them. Also, as we know, a great deal of what they think of as junk is stuff that we can turn into several pounds a go. Sometimes it's hundreds.

But how to get the edge on the 'civilians' (non-dealers) at the sale?

Which Sales?

First, KNOW YOUR SALES. Good sales are The Scouts, Women's Institute, Conservative Party, Guide Dogs, and Country Churches. They have three things in common – MONEY (wealthy members), STRONG

ORGANIZATION (lots of stuff collected), WIDE APPEAL (lots of stuff donated for popular cause). Any two of these gives you a winner sale. With all three, like The Scouts, it's a BRAHMA.

Sales to avoid are Nursery/Play/Infants Schools – the small kids, no-dough syndrome again. Also, amateur dramatic societies – they're all crooks and fornicators, wouldn't give away the drips off their nose (Pat's words, not mine). Also, 'Green' outfits and crackpot political groups – all knitted toys and ethnic shite. Also, Easter/Christmas 'fairs' where most of the goods are home-made stuff from egg cartons and yoghurt pots – useless to a dealer.

The Wooden Horse

When you've sorted out the sales worth doing from the newspaper adverts (again – no advert, no show), you prepare a 'wooden horse' for each one.

This is a largish, cardboard box filled with what looks like good gear but is in fact worthless. You include broken, unrepairable stuff, torn or stained clothing carefully folded to look good, religious books not worth more than 10p each. You make up a good box of what would normally go in the bin.

Arrive about an hour before sale time. If it's a good sale, a queue will have already started, with the smart-arses sitting on the step two hours before. They think they'll get the bargains but haven't reckoned for the 'raiders' like us.

You go straight in, trying not to look too dealerish if you can, and present your box of goodies as a contribution to the sale, like you were Lord or Lady Bountiful. All you're giving away is the biggest load of crap since dinosaurs had diarrhoea – but it will be received with polite thanks.

Now you are in the enemy camp, you can preview all the goodies at leisure and note the position of the best stuff on the table. You're looking for 'hard goods' only – antiques, electricals, paintings, pots and glass, silver etc. Ignore clothing, books and toys, except old or tin-plate toys which fetch big money at present.

If you're a real pro, you get talking to someone and offer to help behind the tables. They think you're a supporter because you brought in a contribution.

While you are helping out, you slip one or two good bits of 'tom' (jewellery) or other antiquey bits in your pockets. Most jumbly organisers are too hysterically busy to notice what you're at.

The Find (One of Pat's Inventions)

One of the great tricks is the 'find'.

If there's something real tasty, don't jump at it but pick on something else, oldish, and say 'Here, this is worth quite a bit, you know'. Tell the tale that an aunt had one like it and it fetched, say, £20 at auction, They'll be impressed and one greedy sod among them will withdraw it from sale and promise to take it for valuation next week.

When you offer to give a 'jacks' (£5) for the real tasty bit, they won't suspect that it's worth a 'oner' (£100) or more because they trust you by now. You get a nice touch while the mugs are still queueing.

A good raiding team can clear everything worth having from a sale before it starts and pay little more than the price that would have been asked over the table when the mugs come in.

If you can't stay in the hall, have a 'number two' (accomplice) queue early. Do the wooden horse, then come out and decide between you which bits you're going for when the tapes go up. You're streets ahead of the opposition cos you know the lay out and just what you are after. No time will be wasted in getting your bearings.

The Big Bag

When you go in like this, it gets real dirty. Normal law-abiding folk turn into monsters to get a bargain – so again you need an edge.

First, carrying power. You can't afford to have your hands full, so you have big bags and pockets. The best bag is one from a shopping trolley, taken off the frame. It will fold up under your arm and drop open as you run to the tables. It won't burst like a bin liner and holds as much as Santa's sack.

Diversions

At the table, there is a mass of folk tearing at the stuff, desperately trying to find a bargain. You need something to slow them down – a diversion.

A old lady fainting is a cracker. It's not difficult to make sure one goes down. No. 2 drops something on her right. He bends down. You stumble against her, like you were pushed. The old lady tips over your No. 2 man, soft like. The crowd is frozen by the fall. Chaos – which makes a good cloak for cunning.

The good folk behind the table come forward to help (don't want no trouble – could it be a heart attack?). You and No. 2, back on feet, sweep goodies into the big bag like it's Christmas.

If you haven't the heart for the old lady, go for an old boy. A good knee in the goolies will give all the appearance of heart failure and no one will notice the dirty deed in the crush.

A kid screaming, cos of a sound elbow in the ear, is a good show stopper too.

The Penguin Swipe

Another good touch is the penguin swipe. Keeping your left arm by your side, grab your target item with your right hand and sweep it under your left armpit. No. 2 pulls it out from behind and into the bag. Practised, the movement is so fast that no one sees it. You've held the item for a fraction of a second and it's gone. Stage conjurers use a similar move to 'disappear' things. Your bag, held by No. 2 should be full in less than three minutes. No. 2 gives you the 'tap' on the back to go, and you should be out and away to the next do in five.

Straight Dealing – Pat Style

If there's a lot of big stuff you've got marked for having, grab the first one and push it under the table. Then ask the server to hold it 'at the back', giving her a pound. Experienced servers know you are dealing and will accept the pound as a sort of down payment on a number of items all of which go 'over the back'. You haggle the bulk price when you've got all you want.

You make it fast. Offer a fiver when you know it's a tenner's worth and No. 2 is clearing it before the deal's done. They won't miss the bits he is putting inside other things.

A good team practises these moves at home – so they go like snot off a stick at a sale. That's why you with your inexperienced eye rarely see the moves. It's all too quick. The raiders are away with a oner's worth or more before you pay your first ten pence for something worth five pence. Of course you need the 'eye' to know what's worth a tenner for ten pence.

Now, you might think this sort of trickery is petty and mean. But it's not the odd pound or so that counts. IT'S TIME. While you're giving the old gal behind the table 10p, you're losing good bits to another raider, or worse to a civilian who doesn't know the value and would waste it. At a good sale you find small collectables that will fetch from 10 to 50 pounds. Our three minutes or so 'at the front' could be worth a couple of hundred quid, so we don't waste time paying ten pences and losing out.

I've often tossed a jacks to a seller, or given it to the door minder as we leave, so that they're not 'out' on the deal. Valuable 'little bits' can't go 'at the back' – they'll get broken or nicked by another raider before you can collect. It really is that vicious when this sort of money is involved.

Regular jumbly organizers aren't 'green'. They know what goes on but never try to develop an 'eye'. They've probably got too much money to bother.

Amateur Auctions

The wide ones are increasingly moving toward amateur 'auctions' rather than jumblies. They get their mates to put in dummy bids to bump up the prices. I know this for a fact because I often act as auctioneer at these do's.

I charge 10% of the 'take' and usually get a few bits for myself before the viewing starts. So we win and the punters and civilians lose every time.

The organizers know I've got the 'brass' to take bids 'off the wall' (pretend that bids are coming from the crowd). This, done well, is better than dummy bidders and gets everything sold for good prices. But it needs the experience that organizers don't have.

———

Nasty stuff eh? But 'Penguin' is a wealthy man from raiding and booting. I know of several tasty bits that he got for pennies which sold at auction for more than a grand. One piece of Delft pot made three. Judge Pat as harshly as you like, but remember that there are baddies on both sides of the jumbly table.

The Other Side

Just watch sale organisers weeding out good bits, not to sell for their cause but for themselves, with the cynical remark 'I'm not giving that away'. They then wait smugly for the mugs to rush in, despite the fact that some are now charging as much as £1 admission.

I've often heard this conversation too:

'We might get £5 for that.'

'But it doesn't work.'

'Oh, that's alright. It's all for charity and it makes up for what gets stolen!'

Seen from this angle, Pat seems just a little less of a crook. Who corrupted whom is academic.

Charity Shops

Our next source of stock is the charity shop.

Once a soft target, they have 'grown up' with the boot trade and most are now pretty sharp. Items suspected of real value are sent off for expert opinion – usually by an auctioneer who advises for free, just as he will for you if there's a chance of selling for you and making his commission.

But plenty of goodies still slip through the net. Though shop managers can be on the ball, their help usually consists of unpaid volunteers. If you pay peanuts you get monkeys and if you pay nothing you get nothing – that's the kind of knowledge your volunteers are likely to have. Good things often go unidentified into the dustbin.

Green booters just visit the shops. Sharp cookies check the dustbin when the shop's closed – but that's against the law unless you get permission first. I've fished plenty of good stuff out of charity shop bins with the manager's consent. Also that's where your wooden horse material comes from on Friday nights. Two birds, one stone – see?

As a known dealer, the shops will ask my opinion on stuff and hold back likely looking bric-a-brac that an auctioneer will consider a waste of his time. I buy this sort of stuff in bulk and also broken things that can be repaired. More on repairs and refurbs in another chapter.

Some 'charies' (shops) can be snotty to dealers – so you aim to get stuff from their bins. It's their loss if they're too dignified to deal.

Most see you as a friend who will increase their turnover. They are as much in biz as me and they get their stock for nothing too.

You deal with charies on a weekday when it's quiet and then only deal with the shop's principal. One dealer got caught out buying stuff from a volunteer helper who was pocketing the cash and they both got busted for theft.

The manager may be on the fiddle – not unknown! Well, as they say, 'who guards the guards?' One shop manager made twenty grand like that before he got too greedy and was caught. He was weeding out the good gear and booting it on Sundays. The shop takings plummeted. Someone smelt a rat and the inevitable trap was set.

Fund-Raising

While we're on charity in general, here's a lovely touch. The fund-raising system.

You go see your local deserving cause, football club or whatever – not a national thing but a local one – and offer to raise funds. If you're credible, they jump at the chance of a few quid. Next get a couple of thousand leaflets run off something like this:

ANYTOWN BOY'S FOOTBALL CLUB FUND RAISING APPEAL
DO YOU HAVE ANYTHING WE COULD SELL TO RAISE FUNDS?
WE WILL TAKE ANYTHING – JUNK, BROKEN, WORN OUT OR WHATEVER.
WE DESPERATELY NEED FUNDS. DON'T BIN IT, LET US TAKE IT.
WE WILL BE CALLING ON XXXX (DATE)
THANKS FOR YOUR HELP etc, etc.

Get the pic? Don't go spending money on photocopying or printing. Get an old duplicator for a fiver or so. You see them at boot sales! The more amateur the leaflet the more credible the appeal becomes and you breed sympathy. Put out your leaflets locally, wait a few days and then collect as promised.

You will be AMAZED by the response. Boxes and sackfuls of stuff will often be waiting on the doorsteps. I was given a whole houseful of stuff once. If you put a phone number on the leaflet you will get calls to pick up stuff. Amongst the haul will be at least one item worth a lot of dough.

Work out the value of the stuff and give 10% of the take to your cause. They will be delighted cos they did nothing to get their windfall except give you credibility.

It costs you next to nothing, bar a little work, to make the lion's share. You can do it all again next year. Half a dozen like this every year and you are on the way to the sort of dough city whizz kids used to make – and it's legal!

A word of warning! If you are given cash contributions, make a note of the donor's name and address and pass the money and details on to your cause. If there are a lot of these, you can reduce the 'donated' percentage of cash realised from the sale and still look like a millionaire philanthropist.

People have earned knighthoods like this and you are being paid handsomely to do it – stock for nothing, see? Your cred in society rises. You are respected as a good guy/gal, and all the time you are getting richer by the minute.

Self Promotion

Build on your reputation. It all helps in dealing. The more folk you know, the more you make.

Never deny that you are in biz. It's no crime to make a profit. People admire success – particularly in those who don't mind getting their hands dirty. How many times have you heard this? 'He deserves it. He works hard and he's been good to us.'

I have a reputation for giving a lot of money to charity. I don't boast but let rumour do the job for me. The money was never mine in the first place and I spent no more than a fiver to make it happen. My reward was in hundreds.

Due to my reputation for helping a local club, its chairman asked me to arrange the disposal of a deceased relative's effects. He felt he could trust me more than a stranger. I quite fairly charged a modest commission of 10% and made over £3,000! When he insisted on giving me another £500 for the work, I donated it to his club and became an idol! I could do no wrong. I made endless good contacts from that little situation and they earned me far more than the extra 'monkey' he pressed upon me.

Losing Dealers

Not all dealers earn good money. Some could fall into a pit of diamonds and come up holding a knob of coal; but they still can't stop trying.

It's easy to be a 'losing dealer' and the basic fault is lack of knowledge. It doesn't require a lot of brains to deal, just the ability to take in facts as you're doing now. But some can't or won't learn.

Alan's Story – How Not to do It

Let's take Alan. Al has been on the circuit for years and is just as poor now as when he started. He began in booting ten years ago, selling stuff from jumblies. He never learnt jumble raiding but just stood in the queue and took his chance. He hadn't got the nerve to 'ride the wooden horse' so never got the good stuff.

His image was 'loser' – glum expression, down at heel and dowdy.

Pulling £30 or so from Sunday boots, he decided to go to junk auctions for stock. He borrowed money and bought job lots heavily. He then had to rent two lock-up garages to store his stock – more expense! Instead of selling as he bought, he hoarded stock and got his store burgled more than once and, of course, couldn't afford to insure!

His stock deteriorated in damp conditions and Al could never find time to prepare it for sale, having had to take a part-time job to pay his borrowings back. He then decided to go full market trading. 'That's where the big money is,' he reckoned.

Things got worse; He paid a lot of dough for a fancy flash and ran up more debt with the H.P. on a big van. A run of bad weather depressed market trading and Al, who didn't know how to buy at wholesale anyway, was in serious trouble. The landlord wanted back-rent for the garages (he still had old stock there). The H.P. wanted payment for the van.

Al was still doing a part-time job and running to catch up, using the van to store his market stock. Then the van was stolen. Well, what did he expect when he left it outside a block of council flats, fully loaded? The van was insured, but not the stock or the flash. To cut a long story short, Al came to me and told his tale. He needed money like NOW.

We went to the garages, which were packed solid with job gear and jumbly stuff. It took hours to sort out but there was some good stuff. Even jumble mugs can buy good bits by accident but Al hadn't the eye to recognise it.

I gathered enough for a booter the next Sunday and, in the meantime, organized a job sale in a hall used by one of my charity clubs (which they very kindly let me use for nothing). I had to drag Al out of bed for the booter at 6 a.m. on Sunday – he always turned up late and got a bad pitch – and we took a reasonable £150, more due to bulk than quality.

The job sale, which I advertised around the trade as an 'emergency clearance' did well. I had Al and family cleaning all the stuff and lotting it up in fresh cartons from the supermarket skip. It all looked good gear on the night and the 300 odd lots fetched a couple of grand. It was rubbish, of course, but all good booter/dealer stuff and well presented.

A sharp dealer could have cleared Al's stores for nothing, the way he was on the ropes, but even I couldn't hurt this dozy but likeable bloke. I split the take 50-50, after giving a 'oner' (£100) to the club for the hall.

The insurance eventually cleared the H.P. on the van, which turned up wrecked some weeks later. The stock was not found, naturally, and nor was the flash. Al was back to square one. I don't think he ever paid the landlord who was glad to have him out and get in a paying tenant.

———

Learning from Mistakes

What can we learn from Al's mistakes? I bet you could tell me!

Turn stock fast. Never hoard without good reason, like increasing value in antiques or collectables, waiting for a special punter or a spare part to make good. Don't be a jumbly mug. Learn at least a basic 'eye'. Don't try the big time before you have the small time right. Learn your trade. If you're a dealer – deal! Don't fall back on part time work for peanuts.

Job stuff out at small profit if things are tight, for there's always more where that came from. Get your kip and be out early for sales. The trade doesn't owe you a living unless you turn up to receive it.

Don't incur useless overheads like storage for goods you should have cleared. NEVER leave goods on a vehicle unless you're loaded for an early start. Have your wagon virtually thief proof, bristling with alarms or SLEEP IN IT! And of course, don't be a losing dealer. Be part of the trade, not a party to it.

Al wasn't suited to the game. He wasn't a social bloke nor was he really hungry for money until he got into debt – then his worries pulled him down in a spiral of failure. Watch for warning signs of this sort of thing. When you spot them, stop and think what you are doing wrong. You detected Al's mistakes so don't make them yourself, O.K?

Trying Out

We'll look at other stock sources later, but it's worthwhile trying out jumbly technique before you move on. You'll learn a lot and soon get recognised as one of the fraternity when you make regular appearances. Other dealers are not enemies and you'll soon find 'comrades in arms' among them. Dealers actually help one another a lot as long as you show a friendly spirit and a willingness to reciprocate without being a soft touch like Al.

There are some really nasty types about who will do anyone down, but they get no help and are usually 'frozen out' (ignored) by genuine dealers. If you learn the game and observe the ways, you will be accepted and respected in the biz. Don't be afraid to admit a lack of knowledge. Dealers in the main like to air their ability and show off a bit. Ask and, often as not, you'll get a free lesson in a particular field of goods or trading. Dealers are proud of their trade and its traditions and like to pass them on.

Having mentioned certain types of dishonesty, and there are more further on, I think this is a good time to cover some aspects of the law relating to dealing. So the next bit will cover authority's attitude to the trade and how to stay out of trouble.

Chapter 4
Booting and the Law

The Law

I'm not going to be 'Everyman's own lawyer' here. A little knowledge is a dangerous thing and my knowledge of the law is microscopic. But there are a few odds and ends that it is best to be aware of so that you can stay out of trouble. Not that the law poses any problem to the booter – far from it.

Car booting is entirely legal. Although local and parish councils can get a bit hot under the collar over large boot sales in their area, their objections stem mainly from parking problems and advertising signs and not from the actual sales activities of the dealers on the ven. The booter need not concern himself with these issues until he considers becoming a promoter (see Chapter 12).

The Police

They tend to give boot sales a wide berth unless actually summoned to deal with a problem. This is EXTREMELY rare.

Promoters want everything peaceful and, in the main, steward their events well. I can recall just one occasion in many years when it was necessary to call policemen to a ven – and this was over a matter that had no connection with the sale itself.

Traffic movements can cause problems to police; but these are usually resolved by discussion on traffic management between police and the promoter. The police often advise on ways of improving traffic flow and supply cones to prevent obstructive or dangerous parking.

I have heard a senior policeman describe boot sales as 'havens of crime'. This is a bit of an over-reaction. I can honestly say that I have not heard of one single instance of murder, major robbery, or insurrection at a booter. A better description was coined by a local sergeant who described them as 'a lot of artful dodgers, all trying to catch one another for fun'. Sounds about right, eh?

Certainly, plain clothes officers do mix with the crowds at boots as they do at most street markets from time to time. They're on the look out for blatantly offered stolen goods, for pickpockets, and for 'Three Card Trick' operators. Detectives have little interest in straightforward junk, though they might take a look at newish T.V.s and videos or at jewellery.

I may be naive, but I've never seen a booter being questioned about his stock by a policeman at a ven, nor have I seen drugs being sold. I was once asked to watch for certain items being offered, and have seen a forged note passed and was able to give a description of the passer. That is the sum total of my experience of police activity at boots. Most other booters report a similar level of experience.

I was once told by a policeman that his attitude is 'no complaint, no offence' and there are a surprisingly low number of complaints from boot sales. Most concern lost property or cars stolen whilst attending as a punter – and that happens everywhere today.

The average boot sale is a fairly disciplined affair. People tend to behave themselves pretty well when compared to what goes on at football matches and pubs. They create few problems for the already overstretched police force.

Trading Standards

I won't go into too many details here. In general, the Trade Descriptions Act applies equally to new and to secondhand goods. Responsibility falls upon the Local Weights and Measures Authority or the Trading Standards Office to enforce its provisions.

Trading Standards are making themselves felt at charity shops, auctions and secondhand shops, where they are enforcing regulations concerning the quality of electrical goods, gas appliances, foam-filled furniture and even the eyes in teddy bears.

So far, they have given boots the Nelson's eye. The reason is that, in practice, they find it too difficult to make a case. At a booter you can claim to be selling your own stuff, which is not classed as trading according to the definition in the Trading Standards' brief 'In the Course of Trade'. To the T.S., it's just not worth the aggro – and again, it means getting up early on Sunday. Thank you God for everything.

If you are using weighing scales in the course of biz – and who's interested in selling a pound of carrots at a booter? – you can fall foul of the Inspector. But the man don't like working Sundays and avoids booters like the plague. He's looking for proper traders with bent scales. Booters just don't fit the pic.

Sale of Goods Act

This covers civil rather than criminal actions at law. If you are trading, the legislation applies equally to new and to secondhand goods. Again, the Act is hard to apply in practice – as the purchaser must prove that you are in trade.

Customs and Excise

We may see a bit more activity from these folk with the influx of cheap booze and fags from the continent. Though I doubt if anyone's going to set up a boot off-licence. You never know.

An old chap was once selling home-made wine of atomic quality at a country sale. He said you paid for the bottle on a returnable deposit and that the plonk came free. The Customs men took account of his age and warned him off. Pity. It was good stuff!

E.E.C.

Or, European Economic Catastrophe. Thought I'd put this bit in as it's a trendy requirement for any publication concerning trade at present. Yes, even commerce can be a fashion victim.

Much of the increased activity of Trading Standards is due to Euro Regulations. It's the downside of the new free market intended to make Europe one country for the purposes of business.

Whilst British and other European biz types realize that most of the Monty Python style Euro Regs are to keep the chaps in Brussels in a job, many of the small-time Standards Officers and 'Jobsworths' think the world will come to an end if they don't enforce every dot and comma.

What we need is a 'European Attitudes Commission' to educate our 'prodnose' types in the true Continental approach to Euro Regs. In the rest of Europe, the legislation is framed and passed; and the right thing having been done, everybody then ignores it and carries on as before.

It would be interesting to see a British Trading Standards Officer try to enforce a few of the Euro Regs in the Paris Marche aux Puces. Such a brave soul would no doubt hear some quite nasty things said about the Duke of Wellington or King Henry V. Even Hitler's name might get a mention and the Entente would be far from Cordiale. Perhaps when the novelty of all the new-found power wears off, our Standards Officers will relaxez-vous a bit and develop a little European laissez-faire. We can only hope, mes amis.

Sunday Trading Act

This pops up every so often, like the issue of capital punishment. Shops may suffer from occasional action by Local Authorities. As far as car boots are concerned, they might as well try to charge fairies with trespassing at the bottom of the garden or keep miners away from a gold rush.

The last bloke who tried to stop Britain having fun was Oliver Cromwell. He was lucky to die in bed and at his funeral you couldn't get into the graveyard due to the number of people wanting to help fill in the hole.

Children

The law is quite blunt about the employment of children in trade. But again, the booter is a bit different.

If your youngsters are just along for the ride, maybe keep an eye on something for a bit, that's hardly employment, is it? At that rate a child shopping with mum could be said to be employed if it carries a bag.

There are no 'sweat shop' employers at boots and most kids have fun. The only crying is from punters' kids. The kids are as much at risk at a booter as they are helping at a jumble sale. Booters know each other well and know each others' kids. It's like having lots of aunts and uncles.

The Fagins (see chapter 6,) are despised and hated – not so much for theft as for exploitation. They are 'grassed' (informed on), usually anonymously. But more often they just get a beating. I know, two wrongs don't make a right. But sometimes we think with our hearts rather than with our brains.

Bin Diving

This concerns raiding dustbins for saleable stuff. At one time a lot of fuss was made about whether taking something from a dustbin was theft. Just who you are stealing from was a debatable point. It was argued that if the owners put stuff out for disposal then they have cast it to the winds, so to speak. It was said that for something to be stolen it's got to have a value and someone has got to feel deprived of it.

However, there is NO DOUBT that taking anything from a dustbin without the owner's permission is THEFT. It is AGAINST THE LAW and no argument.

The easy answer is to knock on the door of the bin owner and ask for the stuff. Very few refuse you. Some tight types ask for money. Most couldn't care less as long as you don't make a mess. You are unlikely to get into trouble bin diving as long as you are tidy and don't go tipping stuff over the pavement.

The ecological angle has soaked into our psyche and folk, by and large, would prefer their junk to be put to use rather than destroyed.

Bin men have a different attitude. Many do very well from the loot in bins, though the Council or their Waste Contractors will deny this. Bin men are forbidden to 'tot' (retrieve for gain) the stuff – but we're not daft, are we?

Council Tips

At the tips where dust carts disgorge their loads, 'shitehawks' (people who make a living from scavenging at tips) abound and the managers get their cut of the spoils.

Some depots are tied up in illegal agreements between hawk groups and the site employees. Woe betide the outsider who tries to 'pick' (sort through) the stuff. It's not uncommon to find that the hawks are virtually running the show – examining the load on cars or vans tipping and directing the good stuff straight to their own vehicles rather than to the bins.

The visitor is not in a position to argue – for violence is not uncommon amongst the hawks. Dump employees are often too terrorised or get too good a cut to complain. The authorities deny it all.

Unless you are a real 'Rambo' type it is best to stay away, except to dump stuff. I have been asked as a regular tipper 'When are you going to bring something good in?' and told that I will be banned from the site if I don't see the hawks 'right' (give them money), or else bring in good stuff!

That attitude changed when I expressed interest in buying stuff. I was now a customer, so could tip free.

Hawks don't boot much, they prefer to spend all their time at the dump and sell bulk for low prices, for such is the volume of their trade. Weekends are their busy time, so booting would reduce their spoils and leave their source unguarded for another hawk group to take over. Then they would have to fight the newcomers to get back. The tip has become their place of biz and almost their home. They are real outlaws and very aggressive.

Danny is a hawk and one of the few that I could get talking, other than to trade.

Danny's Story

I've been doing the tip since I got sacked from the dust for nicking. You can't turn your back on a good thing. Now the private people have took over it's even easier. The Council blokes used to poke their nose in, but this lot just leave us to it. There's so many of us that they don't want trouble. So long as the stuff gets moved they don't care.

People throw out brilliant stuff. You get near-new stuff all the time. Working tellys and all sorts, motors too.

We sell our stuff to dealers that come here. Antique blokes that have posh shops come an' we get good dosh from them – lots of car booters too.

The cookers an' stuff go to a bloke that does them up for sale – bikes the same. The motors we sometimes use ourselves, but most go to dealers. They're mostly wrecks for spares. The Council sells any good uns it pulls in, so what's the bother about us sellin' stuff? It only goes down the pit if we don't.

A lot of the blokes here have got bother with the law an' that. There's a couple living in a cara (caravan) on site cos they had to get from a proper address – bein' looked for, you know. We have to stay here most of the time cos if not other blokes would try to edge in. If that happens there's a battle an' no messin'. You have to protect the dump cos it's good money an' a good little hide like.

There's no jobs outside an' most of us don't want to do anythin' else.

We're all right here an' we're stayin'. It's our place an' we run it our way. We even wear the same gear (overalls) as the firm's blokes so no one knows we're not workin' for them when they come to tip. They just think it's all part of the thing, saving the good stuff for cyclin' (recycling).

———

A true alternative life style, and another sad comment on Britain in the nineties, but Danny's got a point. Should perfectly good stuff go to waste? I don't mean old wrecked cars, but often, as he says and I've seen, damned near new stuff thrown in the bin. That can't be right, can it?

Skips

The industrial form of dustbin. No problems for divers from builders. It's not just bricks and rubble either. A lot of money can come out of a skip.

You stick your head in to the 'job' and shout 'Can I raid your bin, mate?' The answer is always 'Help yourself, take all you can', cos skips cost a lot of dough to hire. The more you take the more space is left, fewer skips are needed, builders' costs drop and everybody's happy.

But you have to be careful. Some long jobs have their regular diver, who is giving the builders a 'drink' (money, usually) here and there for exclusive rights to dive.

I've had some lovely touches from skips particularly at commercial premises. Where there's a shop-fitting job on, you get spot lights, strip lights, odds and ends of stock. Often the stuff is just a few months old and very expensive commercial quality too.

Industrial and Shop Skips

This is where you have to be a lot more careful. At the rear of most parades of shops there are large skips for commercial waste – and WASTE is the word.

Shopkeepers can be the meanest swines on earth. If they can't shift a line they will destroy it and bin it rather than let anyone have the benefit of it. They are often the laziest swines too. Sometimes they can't even be bothered to destroy the stuff, just bin it. I'm not talking about food past the sell-by date. No one wants that. I'm talking about shoes, clothing, books, toys, anything.

But oh! watch out if you go diving without permission and 'shoppy' sees you. He's furious you might get something for nothing instead of paying his rip-off prices. Don't bother to ask to dive, the answer will be NO. That's the nature of the beast. Bloody mean. He won't even sell it to you cos he can't bear to think you might be able to sell what he got burnt (lost money on) by.

So you take your chance here and can get in trouble if you're caught diving at the back of shop premises – even if the yard is open to access, as many modern developments are. Technically, that's theft.

You do NOT of course go forcing your way into locked yards for that's another offence. But some shops, and not just the little ones, need to have these wickedly wasteful practices exposed.

Factory and Office Skips

More risk here. Manufacturers, convinced they are at the forefront of technology even if they are twenty years behind the times, may take you for an industrial spy. Offices think you might be looking for evidence for the Inland Revenue, or be a researcher for The Cook Report. Is no one honest? But some come round with reason.

I've had some success with factories and offices by pointing out the usefulness of their waste. It's the ecology bit again.

Business is scared stiff of the Green Lobby. The idea of a journalist photographing their waste sends them all wobbly. It's said that there's no such thing as bad publicity. But a business, given the idea that it might feature as the villain in an article on waste, suddenly gets keen on recycling and wants you round every week. I've even advised on better ways to dispose of waste. It's surprising the info you pick up without even realizing it

Get friendly with a big factory or office and you've got a nice little dive, once they're sure you're not interested in paper waste or rather what's printed on it. Soul of discretion me. As I say, I'm only interested in recycling. The expensive camera I carry is just a hobby.

Your Obligations

These are both legal and moral if you are going to be successful in the game. O.K., so a few rules get bent now and then. Come on, we're all adults. But I stop short of all criminal activities which, if I'm to tell you the full inside story, I have got to reveal.

The following is the code of ethics that will keep you clean.

Vehicles

Your transport, however unattractive, should comply with the law. With the money you earn there is NO reason to be using a dangerous or illegal motor. That's just a silly, two-bob attitude.

Stock

Never sell anything, particularly electrical, that you know to be unsafe or dangerous. There have been a number of nasty accidents with boot-sold stuff of that sort, and it's just the sort of thing that is likely to spoil the free and easy nature of booting.

We operate very free from the kind of legislation that most traders have to observe. Let's not spoil a good thing or someone's life for the sake of a few quid, eh?

Bin Diving

Ask and it shall be given. Just tell them you're a 'Green' or you want it for yourself cos you're poor, broke and honest. AND say thank you! Then you can call again, see? It can be done legally and with dignity.

I have many regular calls like this in wealthy areas. I sometimes take the ladies a little bunch of flowers and they're deeply touched by the thought shown. It never occurs that I might have more money than they have. I'm just 'that nice man who asks for odds and ends, so polite'.

I was once asked if I could 'find a use for' two old paintings. They fetched £1500 at auction. Not bad for 50 pence worth of petunias, eh?

Stolen Goods

Never worth the risk. They have to be paid for unless you go stealing – and we can get good gear for nothing without becoming thieves, can't we?

If you're daft enough to go displaying stolen stuff in broad daylight at a boot sale, then you haven't got the brains to be a good booter. More on my rather strait-laced attitude to crime in the next bit where we meet some of the real crooks in the biz.

Chapter 5
All that Glitters

Sharp Practice

Every barrel has its bad apple and every trade its villains. You find bad 'uns in every walk of life, but more so in some trades than in others. There are fields of business where an old-time reputation for sharp practice lingers on long after the act has been cleaned up. In others, it seems that dodgy dealing is almost a tradition that would somehow spoil the whole thing if it changed.

Horse dealing springs to mind as one such. The car has long replaced the horse as the universal mode of transport but, until recently, many of the horse dealers' less desirable practices were still prevalent in the motor trade.

Legislation has squashed what was known in the past as the 'bomb site' dealer; and various organizations concerned with higher standards and improved image have, along with consumer associations and the media, forced a more legitimate and responsible attitude in the motor trade.

This is far from the case in general dealing.

As we saw in the previous chapter, there is precious little legislation to control what goes on in booting. Consequently the trade has become a haven for the type of operator who has been driven out of more legitimate pursuits. It has given rise to its own new breeds of crook.

Of course many of the tricks are just old ideas with new coats of paint; but the newcomer may not even be aware of the 'traditional' methods of dishonesty. So now's the time to 'wise up' before some smart Alec 'has you over', as we say, and leaves you 'holding the baby'.

Stolen Goods

Assuming you are going to operate as cleanly as a genuine dealer can, the last thing you want to do is find yourself offering the unsuspecting public 'hot gear'. It is estimated by one of my more dishonest contacts that something like 20% of the higher price goods at boots are in fact stolen.

You can't be absolutely sure about this but there are ways of making a fair assessment of the 'pedigree' of what is being offered by traders and, more importantly, offered to YOU.

Let's cover the obvious stuff first. Say you are approached at your gaff by two young men in modern sporty gear. They give your stuff the once-over and having waited till it's a bit quiet, one of them leans over the flash and says something like 'Do you ... er ... buy stuff, chief?' Now every one knows that booters buy stuff. What the 'er' means is 'are you interested in stolen goods?' You need to understand the language, see?

The odd one-off item is always difficult to assess, unless it's obviously worth hundreds and is being offered for a few quid. If the thing is brand new or still in its box. then ask 'the questions.'

'Where did you get it?'

'Have you the right to sell it?'

'Can you prove it's yours?'

'Can you prove your address/identity?'

Before you get to question four, the crook will be on his way, usually having insulted you first.

If the stuff is obviously secondhand, your seller will most likely be wanting the sort of price you would hope to get for it, so why bother to buy? As a dealer you can get better stuff for next to nothing, so why get involved in a crummy one-off deal? The best motto is 'If in doubt leave it out'.

Most real crooks have a fence who takes or 'receives' their stolen stuff. If they are having to tout it round boots then they are either small-time and unreliable even by criminal standards, or the stuff is so 'hot' that a fence won't touch it. Neither should you. There is more than enough stock available to dealers without getting into trouble over stolen goods.

Con Men

So, the same two likely lads approach you and make the 'er' offer. Let's just assume that you are daft enough to get interested.

One of them shows you a brand new and expensive electric drill, still in its box, which he has in a plastic carrier with him. The price asked is a fiver. When you show interest, you are told that they have ten more just like it in their motor.

You are now taken into their confidence as one of the thieving brother-hood. Of course, says No. 1 crook, we can't just carry the stuff over to you here. The law might be about. Get someone to mind your gaff and come over to our motor and see the goods. This you do and you're shown the other drills in the motor. Arrangements are made to meet the villains – usually at a pub, after the boot sale has closed, where the deal will be done.

It all happens fast now. You hand over the £50. The drills in their boxes go in your wagon and everyone is away like scalded cats. EXCEPT, when you get home you find the boxes contain old knackered drills of similar weight or, worse still, bricks.

You've fallen for the old 'switcherooney' and are the victim of your own greed and dishonesty.

The crooks sized you up as green, conned you by letting you think you were joining the criminal classes for big profits, and ripped you off nicely. Couldn't happen to you? This trick is worked dozens of times every week. And some idiots are conned more than once by various versions of the trick. These boys are real pros and have their act off to perfection. Are you going to the police to tell your tale?

The same rule applies. DON'T GET INVOLVED WITH HOOKEY GEAR.

Shadow Men

These are booters who have learnt all the arts of improving rough stuff until they get so good they don't bother with a stall any longer.

The art is to get an expensive but totally worn out item of electrical stuff or similar, then work on it till it looks like new. They put it in a box with all the papers, so that it looks as if it came from a shop, and then sell it as stolen gear or personal property (with a plausible story) to some greedy, green mug.

The 'shadow' is usually middle-aged, respectable looking and very plau-sible. The goods look perfect but are in fact useless.

Sold at a stall, they will soon have irate punters back asking for refunds – often accompanied by a 'handy' (violent looking) friend or relative. But how do you find the shadow when he has no stall? They are often as adept at changing their own appearance as they are at faking stuff.

Some say that the shadows enjoy the fun of the con more than the money they earn. This has got to be true when you consider the work they put in, but it's you that loses out if you're shadowed.

Actor Dealers

These guys are the ones who really get booting a bad name. They don't look like crooks and their knowledge is amazing.

Whatever the customer's interest, the actor knows about it. Electronics, antiques, paintings, collectables, books etc. – he knows them all and can hold his own in conversation on the intricacies of each and any one.

His flash is an Aladdin's cave of goodies but every one is dodgy. Fakes, dogs, shadow gear – he's got it all but his line in chat is so plausible that the punter is soon sucked in by this knowledgeable and cultured chap who, in his own words, 'boots as a sort of hobby, really, you know. Something to do since the wife passed on'. He's usually retired from some profession or other, according to him – the army is a favourite.

His prices are low for the quality apparently offered and he sells out fast and leaves early. Irate punters are often seen staring at the vacated pitch of an actor dealer.

He tends to do each site once and then stays away for some weeks till the dust settles.

All his gear is class. Good-make electronics, class 'tom' (jewellery), good porcelain. No junk or odds-and-ends boxes on display. Anything under a tenner is beneath the actor.

It's a class act and the top team is a shadow and an actor working together. They can clear £300 in a couple of hours and be on their way. Not bad when you consider that they probably both have a pension coming in as well.

The Last Minute Bargain

The commonest trick of the cheat. As a venue starts to wind down and stalls pack up, the cheat produces his ace card. A new item, usually a very nice looking T.V. or video recorder, is suddenly and prominently displayed.

It hasn't been on show up till now for one good reason – it doesn't work and would cost a fortune to repair, far more than its value as a working item. Good working stuff like this would be gone in the first hour but, if faulty, would soon be back with a demand for refund.

The punter is told that someone agreed to buy it 'first thing', left a deposit but hasn't come back. The mug thinks that he 'talks' the seller into letting him have it – for the seller looks unhappy in case his original (imaginary) punter turns up.

Mug ends up paying a lot of dough for the 'dog'. The gaff gets cleared away double quick, so it's gone by the time mug has checked the set and found it duff. Mug comes back next week but of course the gaff isn't showing. A month later and the mug's case won't stand up. He could be one of our next fascinating friends.

The Crooked Customers

There are worse animals than those who just steal your stuff – and that is common enough. Forged banknotes, some just colour-photocopies, are passed. It's easier than in a shop. Cash gets stolen from the unwary. And change-twisters abound – 'I gave you a twenty'. But even worse are the following.

Dog Fakers

With the mass of consumer goods in the market, it is quite common to see two of the same item on different stalls at a sale.

The team of dog fakers has a whole van load of dogs. They are usually a family or group who spread out and look for copies of the dogs they have on board. Having located a duplicate, they buy the item and then are back in half an hour, swearing that the good T.V. you sold them is duff. It looks the same set and, unless you are canny and mark goods with an identity, they've got you.

They are a nasty aggressive lot and want their dough back or you are in trouble. The more sophisticated types will complain to the site operator who will, for sake of reputation, give you the option of refunding or being banned from the site.

They usually use two vehicles. A van for the dogs and a car to take back the good stuff so the game isn't sussed. If they do get caught by actually buying a dog it goes into their dog stock.

They are usually travelling types and don't repeat the trick at the same venue more than once a year.

It's a real nasty one but fortunately doesn't happen often. If you are a regular user of a venue and have a good reputation, a venue operator may take your side. But even the best of men don't relish mixing it with a large group of travelling types. There's not much defence against it.

Sardines

This is the term for goods that are useless but saleable.

A good instance is tinned foods that are inedible but with the tins still looking good – hence 'sardines'. The same job lot will circulate among dealers with no one complaining, since they are regarded as a sort of alternative currency. The trouble comes when a novice either opens a tin or sells one as good stuff to a punter.

The range of sardines is vast. From chemist's shop stuff to reels of cotton that a kitten could break, Envelopes with no glue, biros with no ink, a hundred new shoes (all left, size 12), balloons that don't blow up and aerosols that do. Some of the stuff can be a bit dangerous, but only if you use it.

Most comes from job dealers, guys and women who buy up such stuff from manufacturers in millions at prices like ten a penny. It's faulty or mismade stuff and you don't deal in it till you really know the trade.

But if you're clever a sardine can be put to other purposes. I know a guy who bought a thousand wrongly moulded plastic trays, made for bread deliveries, for a hundred pounds. He turned them into front-door shoe scrapers that walked away at £1.50 each in a spell of wet weather. One chap, a farmer, bought a hundred of them five minutes after they went on the flash and asked my chum to deliver another hundred to his farm!

So the sardine can be good and bad according to how you use it.

Unicorn

This is the term for a unique item that looks a bargain but is extremely difficult to get rid of. The true unicorn is rare but certain items have developed unicorn status – the hand operated circular slicer and the Gerry Ratner sherry set come to mind. But even they can be sold, if only for 20p. They're best off as wooden horse material. The real unicorn is superior. It is utterly useless, big, awkward and ugly.

A classic was the fake stuffed camel that an associate (who has asked that I don't name him) bought for £50 in a weak moment. Now you'd think that rarity value alone would move such an object, 'You don't see many of these, guv'. But my chum tried everything to see it off – local paper, that organ of all that is fantastic, Exchange & Mart, the showman's newspaper, World's Fair. Auctioneers laughed at reserve prices as low as £10. It's still rotting away at the bottom of his garden, as far as I know. A wonderful but useless item. A true unicorn.

Several lessons to be learned here. Don't buy unless you know for sure it will sell. Stick to mainstream goods, however boring. Always think of what you might lose before you think of what you might gain. If you take a risk, be sure you can afford the loss. Oh yes, and never believe anyone who says he made a profit on a unicorn. It's as likely as winning the pools!

Boot Pirates

This is more like a disease. We covered it a little bit in chapter 3 and I promised more details here.

Pirating only happens to new booters. It goes like this. You do your very first sale, not quite believing that what you've heard is true. You come home with a hundred quid in cash and can't wait to repeat the exercise. You do it again and it works the second time. You're still not quite sure this is really happening, so you do it the third time with the same result.

You become infected with 'boot fervour' – a desire to get all the junk on earth to turn into cash. This is particularly marked in those who have been very short of money for some time. It is a euphoric state which precedes full blown 'piracy'.

Some new booters have been known to sell everything in their homes, so fascinated are they by the system that turns junk into gold.

Now anyone who has ever thought about our commodity/capital based economy has pondered at least once on why, when you buy a thing in a shop, its value immediately seems to disappear and it's only worth about 10% of what you paid for it – or sometimes near nothing.

These facts come over even harder if you have to sell things to survive. So the person in trouble for money, who discovers booting, develops a kind of gleeful madness on finding that he or she can beat the system and get good money for what the bloke in the secondhand shop down the road wouldn't even look at.

Having sold everything but the clothes they stand up in, the 'fervourish' booters are desperate for stock. Unable to act calmly as THE DAY (Sunday) approaches, panic sets in. They are seen prowling the streets where dustbins are out for collection. Deep in builders' skips, covered in filth, searching for anything to sell, at tips, rubbish dumps and building sites. Nothing that isn't nailed down, padlocked and guarded is safe from them.

They have become PIRATES, prepared to offer anything for sale to get that easy cash. They collect scrap wood and even steal the dustbins themselves. They remove front gates from their hinges and take garden gnomes. They don't see it as stealing – if it's loose it's theirs. All sense of pride or dignity goes as they burrow in any kind of filth for stuff to sell. They look like tramps.

Their gaff, naturally, looks like a scrapheap and so do they. But they are still taking money, that's all they can think of now. Anything can be sold; but as the stuff gets rougher the prices get lower and they need more and more stuff to keep up the take.

A pirate is a natural victim for sellers of stolen goods. All his morals are gone without his noticing it. All that matters to him is that roll of cash in his 'bin' (pocket). He develops criminal, rather than dealer slang. He has brushes with the police over his activities and begins to think of them as enemies, keeping him from his drug – stuff to sell!

The pirate is easy to spot. His gaff is a tip. He wears a filthy boiler suit and is ready to bin dive at a moment's notice. He is dirty with black fingernails and face, matted hair and red tired eyes. He is unshaven.

He will involve his whole family in the biz. His wife will be at the gaff, in worn out clothes, greasy hair and tired expression. The kids will be similar and undisciplined. Everything that comes into the house gets sold through booting. A five pound note is the flag under which this buccaneer sails on his sea of junk.

You may think this an exaggeration. But I swear that I have seen this very thing happen to ordinary decent people when the easy money bug gets them. And I've seen them wind up in court as thieves or receivers just because of it. And that's people who had never committed a crime in their life before they started booting. But they'd never had any money either; and that's the key to it all.

A starving animal will eat itself sick when it comes upon food in abundance. So will a kid when given the run of a sweet shop. Lesson? Don't be a child or an animal.

Booting can be a wonderful living if you keep a cool head and realize that there will always be good stock available to sell at decent prices. There will be a natural dip between clearing your own stuff and bringing in new stock from some of the sources we've looked at and those I've yet to tell you about.

So, read on and don't, whatever you do, become a pirate. All the pirates of old ended up in execution dock and YOU could end up in the dock too! Though you won't actually hang, you could ruin your own and your family's life just for the sake of a little patience. O.K.?

We'll meet lots more bad guys and things later on. But first you need to know more about the punters and the problems they can pose. Also a bit about how to deal with them.

Chapter 6
Great Game but for the Punters

'There's nowt so queer as folk,' as the Yorkshire man said. Once you have had to deal with the general public, you will come to agree with this succinct observation.

Punters (customers), though vital, can be the biggest problem you will ever encounter as a booter. In this chapter we are going to meet the folk who, whilst enjoying themselves in a warped and sometimes spiteful way, have to be dealt with and, if possible, profited from.

No booter, however good at the game, can sell to everyone who inspects their goods. All browsers should be regarded as potential customers – but some are literal ENEMIES! First rule of survival here is KNOW YOUR ENEMY.

Thieves

These, as any policeman will tell you, are everywhere.

Most of the 'nicking' that goes on at boots is of such a petty nature that it's hardly worth bothering about. You don't leave your gaff to chase a thief who's pinched a 50p item. While you're running after them, ten more good bits will disappear from your unguarded gaff – possibly even the cash box! Write off small loses to natural wastage. All traders suffer this; and that bit at 50p probably cost you nothing anyway. It only happens a couple of times at each ven, so why worry?

Good items should always be protected, as I described in chapter 2. Have stuff where you can see it and put expensive things in a showcase.

Fagins

These are a revolting breed and, when the law gets them, they get heavy sentences. Fagins never actually steal but train children to do the dirty work for them.

Always keep a strong eye on a group of kids at your stall. If they act suspiciously, don't hesitate to move them on. Fagin kids make a lot of noise. They pick up things and pass them around amongst themselves and take interest in stuff that does not normally interest children – like good pot or adult jewellery. They pinch stuff they can hide on their persons – not big stuff – though one will ride off on a bicycle you have on display while the others create a diversion.

The Fagin will often have a pitch at the ven where the stolen stuff is sold immediately. They are there to steal and clear the stuff straightaway. They are difficult to catch unless you can positively identify your gear.

Fagins get known by ven organisers who eventually refuse them entry when the weight of complaints builds up. Never hesitate to tell an organiser if you suspect a Fagin operation. They often operate as pickpockets as well. Sounds like Dickens doesn't it? If you don't believe me, ask a policeman.

Definitely

This is another type of small time con, one who looks a bit of a looney.

They approach you with a small dog item, swear you sold it to them as a 'runner' (good working order) and makes a fuss or won't go away until you give over the couple of pounds or so that they 'definitely' gave you. They know that a fuss will turn your punters away and hope you will give them money to leave.

Again, MARK YOUR STUFF invisibly and 'def' has lost. The 'marking' shows them up as crooks or perhaps they've just made a mistake? That's the usual excuse when rumbled.

Ripper and Slipper

Thieves really. Ripper picks a cheap pot or glass item, makes lot of fuss over the deal and then drops and smashes the item just as you are getting his change.

Slipper uses the diversion to pinch a good item – the real target – and slip it in bag or pocket. They move away separately. Slipper is away first while ripper waits a bit to cover the escape by helping clear the mess.

They never hang together at stalls and communicate by prearranged signals. Of course there is no evidence on ripper, even if you notice something missing.

If something breaks, look anywhere but at the 'accident' – especially if it's been paid for!

Dream Boat

He buys a wrecked T.V. or similar for £1 and comes back when he finds it don't work. He expected a full working set for his money!

Your fault! Don't display this kind of rubbish. Need I say more?

The 'Two'

Can be any two adults. No. 1 approaches alone. Picks target item, affecting interest, and then criticizes until you begin to lose faith and consider a severe 'mark down' (price reduction). Then No. 1 goes, leaving you feeling wretched.

No. 1 hovers at next gaff and No. 2 comes to you and offers a low price for same item. You possibly cave in and accept, for you see from the corner of your eye No. 1 moving back toward you. This is a psychological move to undermine your confidence still further.

The 'two' work this trick to get stuff at rock bottom price, usually from 'green' (new) booters. Their victim is often female.

Have confidence in your stock and dismiss heavy critics as time wasters. They soon get the message. The best and most effective answer to the 'critic' is 'I wouldn't buy it then, mate. I'm sure you could do better at another stall'. You are saying 'I know your game and am not daft'.

A bit of fault-finding is a normal part of a deal, but No. 1's performance is given away by his not making a firm offer of anything like a sensible price. At one ven, I watched a 'two' get a £60 chandelier for 75p.

Man and Boy

Like a 'two' but works like this. Man is usually pro dealer. Sends boy to try to buy while he (man) is at next gaff, 'earwigging' (listening to the deal). When boy can't swing deal, man steps in and accuses you of trying to rip kid off. He tries to shame you into a low price.

Again, always suspect a young person attempting to buy adult stuff. Look round for a man when the kid is awkward or too commercial.

Stealers

Stealers are not thieves, but they are sharp – very sharp! They are antique dealers with a shop, or swagmen.

They tour car boots, just as booters are setting up, and try to 'steal' good bits from 'green' (ignorant) booters for a few pence. Once you get known as an efficient booter, they will pass the time of day with you but won't try it on. They will buy stuff though and they love a good haggle.

When you get used to booting, the remark 'The dealers will be round in a minute' will become familiar. It's a daft expression really cos we're all dealers aren't we?

The stealers are just too proud to go fishing in bins or skips. You do the dirty work, then they try to 'steal' your loot. Usually they have a well developed knowledge of antiques – an 'eye'.

They are good for 'off the cuff' second opinions; but be careful!

Mrs Sympathy

She's so poor and would just love that item cos it reminds her of dead husband/sister/brother/mother/dog etc. She's only got 50p left in her purse. She'll even cry and break your heart. She'll call you sir or madam and is so grateful when you fall for this wonderful acting performance and let her have a tenner's worth for ten bob.

She's a real pro dealer but ought to be appearing with the Royal Shakespeare Company. Hidden in her bag is at least £500 in her 'other purse'.

'But she could be genuine' says you. 'Have a heart'. Mrs Symp loves your sort.

The Crying Kid

More tears. 'The strongest warrior can be beaten by a child's cry'. Don't know who said it but it's 'bang to rights' (exactly true).

Nice couple is negotiating to buy antiquey bit. The kiddie she is carrying is quiet, but just when the dealing is getting tough, it breaks into hysterical howling. They press on with the deal and you drop a bit more cos the kid's row is killing sane conversation. You want rid of them but want their dough.

She had pinched the kid or even jabbed it with a hat pin to get their price! Wicked init?

Our Tom

Peculiar to rural areas. Nice old couple have been going over the stock for half an hour. They eventually settle on the first bit they looked at and ask every question under the sun.

When you have already wasted fifteen minutes trying to answer them, you suggest they might like to buy the thing. 'Oh no', says the good lady, turning to her husband. 'But our Tom do have one just like it, don't 'ee luv?'

The only answer I have found to this one is 'They're worth more in pairs'. I wish I could figure out their angle for they never buy anything! You just get used to it.

Which is my Bible

'Green' family group, interested in everything but constantly discussing the possible dangers of each item.

He will ask if you think you ought to be offering those old fashioned deck chairs. 'They can seriously damage young fingers, you know'.

The young son inspects battery operated stuff. 'There are no batteries in this' he accuses. 'You should have a sign saying batteries not included'.

Daughter finds book with pics of zoo animals and starts discourse on the evils etc, etc, etc.

I will leave you to decide, respected student, on the course of action. One of my more tolerant colleagues gets out his prayer mat and begins to salaam to Mecca. He may well be Muslim.

'Y Don't Want That

Husband and wife or sometimes two middle-aged men.

Case 1.

She picks up item. Him: 'Y don't want that'.

This is repeated from one end of the flash to the other, ten or more times. It is repeated at each stall. Just ignore them.

Case 2.

Old boy No. 1 picks up item. Old boy No.2: 'I've got one of them in me shed. I'll dig it out for yer'. This is repeated each time an item is selected by No. 1.

Just for fun I lean over the flash and speak to No. 2. 'Excuse me sir, you don't happen to have the Holy Grail or Glenn Miller's plane in your shed, do you?'

No. 2: 'Wojer mean?'

Me: 'Oh, I just wondered that if you did, you might dig them out for me?'

They usually move on and stop making the gaff look untidy.

I Don't Like it Here

Usually an elderly male, part of a group.

Companions stop to look at goods. Him: 'None of that stuff ever works. It can't be any good at that price. It'll fall to bits the minute you've paid for it. They get special stuff for these places. It's all dodgy. The pattern will wash off. You'll get caught'.

Being a sensitive soul, I usually challenge this type. 'Sir, if you believe what you are saying, why come here at all?'

The answer is usually 'Well, you might find a bargain.'

You figure it out, I can't. His type is nearly always caught by the dog sellers. It's a shame really.

How Do I Know it's Not Stolen?

Often asked in a heavy Irish accent, this one. Although I've always avoided stolen goods, out of devilment I reply blankly: 'Oh, of course it is. You can't get one of these honestly at this price.'

This usually gets a laugh and a sale. I suppose a psychiatrist could explain it all.

Life's Unfortunates

Due to the free entertainment nature of boots, you do increasingly get folk hanging around who make you wonder if they ought to be out alone. It's a sad comment on our society that these folk are left to fend for themselves when they should be properly looked after. They can, and it's not their fault, be a nuisance.

I keep a 'goody box' of small bits, sweets and things to give them. You may say I'm patronising but it's better than telling them to clear off as some callous types do.

I often think that if the rest of the problems listed above finally send me over the edge, I might appreciate a kind word rather than a kick in the pants. But that's just me. You have to make your own mind up on this one.

Others

The above are the main problem customers. You will find others and learn from experience how to deal with them. You'll be relieved to know that the 'aggros' comprise a very small percentage of your trade and most folk are quite reasonable in their dealings.

It's best to keep things light and make a joke of difficulties. Never let an aggro wind you up, it's not worth it. If someone is a pain, get rid of them. There's plenty of good punters so why waste time?

Haggling

Not a traditional British way of purchase but a growing practice at boots.

You price your stuff to take account of an offer. Always price stuff about 25% higher than the price you want to get. Don't be taken in by the punter who says that a seller 'over there' (indicating vaguely across the ven) is offering the same goods at a quarter of your price. Suggest that the competitive item is possibly a fake/doesn't work or is faulty/might be stolen and end with 'There's got to be something wrong at that price. Is that why you didn't buy it, sir/madam?'

This is sales psychology. You compliment the punter with having the sense not to buy something that is obviously too cheap or risky and at the same time persuade them to agree that your price is right. It's a con for a con and all part of the fun – another form of haggling.

Pricing

Some booters say price everything because punters shy away from un-priced stuff. A good point.

Others price almost nothing, particularly if they specialize in antique stuff. The reason for this is that 'ant' (antique) sellers do a lot of biz with other dealers.

Their labels are usually in code which indicates their buying price as well as the selling price, which will differ for trade or civilian punters. These prices will vary enormously according to the quality and authenticity of the item. A pro dealer will know an 'iffy' (fake) antique. Joe punter may not. But more on the ant trade in chapter 10.

Another good reason for not pricing every thing is a practice know as 'sizing up.'

Sizing Up

You do need to have a bit of experience under your belt to be a good 'sizer'.

The theory goes like this. Certain types of folk will pay a good deal more for an item than others will pay. So it's better not to price those things that should be priced according to who's asking and are actually being held back for the right mug with more money than sense.

This theory can apply to many items. Let's take an example. You've picked up by chance a book on railway trains published in the 1930s. It has got some nice pictures and someone might buy it for their train-mad kid for say 50p, not knowing its real value.

To a railway enthusiast, the book's worth a lot more. You could take it to a specialist dealer who would pay about a third of its value, say £5. You could place it with an auctioneers and wait about a year until they hold a specialist sale – but the sale might carry duplicates and you have to pay commission.

SO... You wrap it in cling-film or plastic and wait for the MUG, leaving the book well displayed but UN-PRICED.

Collecting freaks are easy to spot. They can't hide their excitement at making a find. When you see that look of reverence, the almost loving gentleness with which they handle the item, you've got one. They ask the price, expecting a shock. They know you know the value by the way the book or whatever is wrapped.

If they want to inspect it, bring them round your side of the gaff to examine it, perhaps in the shelter of the motor hatch.

The book's worth £15 – you know that cos the specialist dealer offered £5. You ask the fanatic for £30 cos you know he'll settle for £20 with a haggle. See? To him the price is only dictated by how much he's got. Your job is to get as much of it as possible. Play hard to get. Once you've got him hooked, he might not buy straight off. He might walk away. KEEP YOUR NERVE. The best price is always obtained from the punter who comes back in an hour or so to re-negotiate. They've possibly been to the cash machine for more funds!

The same applies to 'ant' and collectables. But here you price according to how much dough you think the punter has, NOT what the item's worth. How do you tell? We'll cover that in chapter 10, cos ant and collectables is a specialized subject.

Now on to money as a commodity, rather than just earning it.

Kites (Cheques)

NO NO NO. Not ever. Never!! At boots it's CASH ONLY. Even with a banker's card they can be dodgy.

If punters really want the goods they will pay cash. No one comes to a boot without cash. They know the score. IF PUNTER HAS JUST HAGGLED AND THEN ASKS TO PAY WITH CHEQUE THE ANSWER IS NO. THE CHEQUE WILL BOUNCE.

If you don't believe me, take a chance and weep. And NEVER accept a cheque from the punter who says 'I'll take that' and whips out a kite without even asking for discount. He's a 'FLYER' (passer of dud cheques). Hence 'flying a kite'. His is another way of getting stock for nothing!

I have accepted foreign currency from time to time, but you have to know your exchange rates and what is acceptable. Check with the bank. Teletext carries exchange rates daily, so do the better newspapers. I never enter a ven without a good daily paper with me just for this purpose. Foreign dosh is a rare event and can be forged. It's best left alone until you get very experienced.

Credit Cards?

Leave it out. This is getting silly! What was that joke about Sproggit and Sylvester?

Chapter 7
The Secret Laboratory

Being a largely uneducated lad myself – I was always bunking off school to hang round markets – I often pick up bits of info but can't always give the source.

I think it was Faust who sold his soul to the Devil for the secret of turning lead into gold. He didn't get much of a deal as I recall. The secret of turning junk into money has been known by the dealing and particularly the booting fraternity for a long while and they didn't pay near as much for it as did Faust.

We don't actually turn junk into gold – what a surprise, says you – but we do turn junk into what LOOKS like gold and get gold, well cash, for it. One of the secrets is appearance. The other is why folk throw good stuff away.

Back in your mother's or possibly grandmother's time, when a woman's work was never done, folk knew how to clean things. They also valued things cos there wasn't a lot about and what they had got had to last.

Today all the drudgery of cleaning is done by machines but little thought is given to the welfare of the machines themselves, bar a wipe over with a damp cloth. Modern plastics and other surfaces need minimum cleaning – so the shops say to sell them – and this suits the housewife of the nineties very well.

Why then does that two-year old vacuum cleaner look such a wreck and get replaced with a new shiny model? Answer: cos plastics may well SEEM to clean easy with a squirt of 'all purpose cleaner'; but in fact, they build up a coat of static goo that your aerosol and duster won't remove. Soon the shiny cleaner looks horrid with black scuffs and marks that won't come off. Mrs 1930 would have known how to treat the problem – but Mrs 1990, born in an era of 'quick clean' doesn't. Out goes the not so old faithful and in comes the new and shiny, courtesy of the credit card.

The scene now changes to Any Street on dustbin day. Rejected vac stands by bin waiting for the tumbril to the guillotine. But all is not lost! In the nick of time the Scarlet Pimpernel snatches condemned vac from the jaws of the dustcart and off to the secret laboratory. Sorry about all this drama, but it does feel a bit like this.

Mrs 1930's methods come back into use. Quick strip down of the loose bits. Tools etc. go in a tin bath full of strong bleach solution. Vac body gets a thorough scrub with same, inside and outside. A Brillo pad is used on tough bits. Cable is cleaned with bathroom cleaner. Fresh paper bag is inserted. The vac is polished and there you go, thirty quids' worth, good as new.

'Hardly been used sir, clean as a whistle'. A light spray of matt black cellulose on the brush-bar covers the wear – most dustbin vacs are working but filthy. Cleaning time? 20 minutes. Cleaned in bulk they take even less time. Selling time for a good un? 1 to 2 minutes. On a good dustbin day you'll pick up 3 to 5 machines.

Non-runners are often just a matter of a fuse gone in the plug or a damaged cable connection. The current price charged by service engineers deters folk from calling them in or taking machines for repair. It's easier to buy new. What's a hundred quid on the old card or from the catalogue? Probably cheaper than a repair. Or they could go to the boot sale – there's a bloke there has them like new for £30!

It doesn't take long to learn to strip cleaners. Best models are Hoover, Electrolux and Goblin – very easy to work on. Some of the more obscure stuff, particularly French, are best avoided unless they just need cleaning. Total failures (motor gone) you sell to the shadow men (see chapter 5) for a fiver or so. They love dogs.

I bulk my vacs up. When I have about 20, I get an electrician chum to check them for safety – takes 5 minutes each one – so I can offer a safety certificate (higher prices). I let 'sparks' have anything he fancies from stock as payment. Costs me near nothing but makes my vacs very attractive buys. I always have 3 or 4 on display in front of the flash. They rarely come home with me.

Most small electrics will respond to the 'scrub up treatment' BUT NEVER IMMERSE THE ELECTRICAL PARTS IN WATER. Just scrub damp. You'll soon get the knack and be turning out near-new stuff from dustbin 'orphans'.

Laboratory Equipment

Best bought from cleaning equipment suppliers, which is where cleaning firms get their gear.

Shopping List

Industrial bleach, in 5 litre containers.
Non scratch cleaning cream, large size. Get a couple.
Soap filled wire wool pads, large size box.
Sponge cloths, packs of 20.
Plastic scouring pads, as above.
Nylon dishwashing brushes, packs of 10.
Bottle brushes, selection of sizes.
Rubber gloves, washing up type, packs of 10.
Disposable polythene gloves, packs of 20.
Clean and shine, large size, say 5.
Polishing cloths, bags of 10.
Paint. Motor spray cans are best. Cellulose will dry in seconds and looks a pro finish. Don't buy from motor shops, except end of line colours (very cheap at about 50p each). Job dealers can supply bulk mixed colours at nothing prices a box full.

The whole lot will cost about a third of shop price. You can, at the start, get the stuff from the supermarket in small amounts but you'll soon move on to commercial purchasing.

Scrubbing Up

I've not done my own scrubbing up for years now. If you're in a big way of biz you have to delegate. My 'scrubber' is Sid. Sid is about seventy, an ex Royal Navy man who knows all about old fashioned cleaning methods. I met him at a booter, where he remarked on the smart turnout of my stock. I asked if he was interested in a few quid on the side.

To be brief, Sid and occasionally his old 'oppo' (mate) Harry, do all my cleaning and preparation work. I provide a good fry-up breakfast, free tobacco, all materials and £15 a day. In return, they work like demons and prepare as much stuff as I can find. Sid picked up the tricks in no time – disguising damage with those small, car touch-up paint pens, super-gluing broken plastic. You get super glue in large size bottles from builder's merchants – not those silly little tubes that cost a fortune.

Plastic Repairs

Here's how you repair broken plastics.

Take, for example, a modern upright cleaner with plastic handle and body. It's had a fall downstairs and the handle is broken from the body. Not repairable says the shop. Don't you believe it. We have the technology! Here's the process:

1 Strip and clean but DO NOT POLISH.
2 Assemble and check for missing bits of plastic. They are usually only tiny bits and are replaced with car body filler. Dis-assemble broken parts.
3 Smother all broken edges with super glue (never mind what it says on the bottle). Re-assemble, holding whole thing together with electricians insulating or 'gaf' tape.
4 Place repair in front of fan heater on max. heat setting. Heat is the secret.
5 When set, about 15 minutes, remove tape. Job looks a mess. Don't worry. Any surface glue will come off using cellulose thinners and a blunt metal scraper.
6 Run over cracks with small tipped, electric soldering iron. Plastic will soften and re-bond.
7 Replace any missing plastic with filler.
8 Touch in with matching paint pen.
9 When dry, seconds on a warm day, finish with metal polish.

The whole process takes about an hour. With practice you can get as good as the shadow men and present an invisible repair.

You only go to this trouble with stuff that is perhaps 6 months or a year old and will fetch substantial money. A six month old, good brand cleaner is worth £50 – more if you can find an original box. Some are put on the bin in the box they came in! Sometimes the old model is put out in the newcomers packaging. This is the stuff the shadows are always after. A good box and maker's paperwork puts £10 on the price. The machine's new, isn't it? Even a ten year old machine can look like new. A scrub up and it will fetch £20.

Dozy or two-bob booters show filthy, damaged machines for three or four pounds. I buy them up when I can, haggling the price down. In a week or so they will be back, sometimes at the same ven, for £30 or more. I've had the same machine through twice on occasions! I recognise them from my 'mark' in ultra-violet pen.

All household gear will respond to the scrub up. Some booters specialize in particular lines. Here's 'Stan the Spray', a kitchenware specialist.

Stan's Story

I do general boot stuff, but my favourite line is kitchen stuff. Saucepans, fryers, kettles etc. I have a system for refurbishing and turn a large amount of stuff every week.

My stock comes from anywhere – dustbins, skips, jumblies, junk auctions. The bin men bring me stuff in bulk. They used to put 'ally' (aluminium) and metal to the scrap but the price has gone right off lately, so I am a good source of cash to them. I pay them by weight regardless of condition. Works out about 15 pence an item average.

A pan might come in burnt black, horrible, enough to turn your stomach. They go straight in 'the vat' that's a big tub filled with heated water and liquid caustic soda. It's dangerous stuff so you wear all the protective gear. Five minutes in the vat will bring the worst burnt or grease-caked pan up like new. You could spend a month of Sundays trying to clean off the muck by hand. Next they're rinsed in clean water to remove all the caustic and dried.

Non-stick is the big seller, so I coat most pans like this. The pan goes on a little electric ring in the spray shed. When it's hot, I spray with my own non-stick -- a mixture of matt black heatproof engine paint and polymer, which will not mix normally but will fuse together when pressure sprayed on to a hot surface. It dries instantly. I learnt the thing from a magazine about surf boards and how to put on tough slippery surfaces.

Some wicked sods just spray the pans with motor paint but it comes off first time they're used. I've had no complaints. Me and young Del (Stan's son) can turn out a couple of hundred units in a day in our back garden workshop. A good make of fryer with a glass lid can fetch 10 to 14 quid if it looks the biz. Sets of 4 or 5 non-stick sauces about 20 to 25 quid for good makes. You'd pay a hundred or more in the shop for the top brands. Stainless gear fetches fortunes.

Missing handles and knobs are no problem. We've got hundreds spare and they're easy fixed. Wood handles are near white from the vat, so we rub them over with artist's brown acrylic paint and spit. They look just like new stuff. Colour and shine in one go.

The handles of old garden tools come up like this and I spray the blades with non-stick. Del grinds up the edges on the power stone. Good fork and spade set goes about £15. We get 'em for £1 each from the dust boys.

Kettles are de-scaled with citric acid. It's quite safe – you can eat it. Costs about £3 a kilo; that will do 20 kets that sell for £6 to £7 each when they're bright and shiny. You just fill them with water, add the citric and leave overnight. Next day all the scale is gone and they're like new.

The cut-out type are great, cos when the elements get furry they won't work so they go in the bin. Once they're de-scaled they start working again. A nice one in a box can make a tenner as new. I get labels and that from Artie. Sonia, my missus, uses them on the bedding stuff she does.

Sonia's Story

I go round the jumblies and charry shops for sheets, pillowcases, blankets, that sort of stuff. They all get a thorough wash as soon as I get them home, I've got a commercial washer and dryer that Stan got through the trade.

The stuff gets ironed nicely and packed in polythene bags like you see it in the shops, but with Artie's labels. I say they're factory seconds and that's why there's no label on the stuff itself. Tracy, my daughter helps pick out the old label. Well you don't want a 'Made in Taiwan' label giving the game away, do you?

I have my flash next to Stan at the vens so we can work together and our lines sort of complement each other. The kids come with us some weeks – but of course young Del's own thing's building up, so often he has to be home to take phone calls an' that.

_____

'Young Del' is building up a nice line in shadowed cars – old wrecks worked on to look like well maintained, 'one owner' vehicles. There is a big market for cheap, reliable looking vehicles in these hard times. When the bodge repair work is done, Stan, who was once a sprayer in a Midlands car factory, does the 'paint job'.

'But who is Artie?' says you. Good question. Artie specializes in labels and 'sale accessories' as he calls them. He works for a printer and also has a colour 'desk-top publishing unit' (fancy word processor) at home.

He reproduces near, but not exact copies of well known manufacturers' labels that fool mug punters; and he sells them to booters and shadow men. It's very easy if you have Artie's kind of kit. Close similarity ain't forgery you know – but it can give rise to other criminal and civil proceedings.

Sonia, Tracy, Stan and young Del have two houses – one in a better suburb of Birmingham and the other a nice cottage in Dorset. They also have three caravans that they let out in summer, a boat that cost £10,000 and three cars. Artie drives a new Jaguar and takes holidays in places like Antibes and Monaco. He's currently courting a minor movie star. He's tried printing money, just for fun; but says it's too risky and there's more dough in labels.

The Alchemists

Dave and George are alchemists. They make stuff like disinfectant, washing up liquid, shampoo, hand cream, cosmetics, anything you like, from simple recipes or formulas that they bought from an ad in a trade mag.

The stuff's poor quality but does the job and is sold in large size containers that make it look a bargain with the nice labels on them. These lads are really manufacturers, but sell direct to the public at boots, so all the profit is theirs – no middle men. Their other lines include kitchen and toilet rolls – poor quality job lines from dealers.

Five litres of wash-up costs them 10p to make and sells for £2. They get the containers secondhand. God knows what was in them before. Probably atomic waste. What do they care? Last year's turnover was £150,000.

Micky 'The Mouse'

Mick is a hi-fi and video specialist. He got the nickname 'Mouse' recently when he moved into computer games and other high tech 'toys'. His stuff looks good and modern though most comes from the bailiff's auctions and is often in a bad state. Sometimes it is 'stolen and recovered legally' and sent to auction by the police, unable to trace the owner. It is often damaged, but is improved by the heavy cleaning and touch-up system.

Mick's partner is Gareth, a qualified electronics engineer. Gareth can bring to life a dog T.V. by shocking the dud tube with a massive high voltage charge which will give a few weeks more life or brighten the picture on a dying set. Low amplification stereos can be made into ear busters with a few little additions, but they don't last long. The addition of a good-make name, stuck on where the cheap one was, ensures a quick sale. There is more ignorance amongst hi-fi buyers than in any other field bar antiques. A good label and shiny appearance does the biz.

I must make it plain here that putting a false label on goods is fraudulent. Don't even think of doing it. There are enough honest ways to make money!

One of the wicked tricks that 'Mouse' showed me is speakers. A large but poor quality pair of speakers is dolled up to look like a good make. A brick is put inside to give the impression of heavy magnets (the sign of quality). The case is re-sprayed in modern finish, black ash over the old 70s teak. A jack plug socket (only found on better makes) is fitted where the wires once entered. A 'top-make' label, one showing a high wattage and lots of techno nonsense, replaces the original. The back is glued on to slow down discovery of the trick. Dog-ish speaks, from charry shop or two-bob booter, cost £2 to £5. The fakes sell for up to £100!

Mick also carries a nice line in pirate video and sound tapes, recorded on top class dubbing equipment at home. True-blue movies are available under the counter to the plastic mac brigade. Videos are a big seller, but you can't shift any colour but black. The silver cases of older models are taken over to Stan's for spraying the saleable colour. Gareth doctors control buttons etc.

Other Industrialists

In some areas, booting and associated operations are almost a neighbourhood industry. A whole network of dubious trade relies on the black economy.

Kev, a mate of 'Young Del', recuts tread into bald tyres for the 'shadow cars'. This is a criminal practice, but very common. Del knows where to get M.O.T. certificates for cars that couldn't pass a kid on a three- wheeler bike, let alone a test.

Just down the road, Peter produces gold chains for the boot jewellery biz. They look like gold and feel the right weight. They're hallmarked too. The marks are put on by a bloke that made his own stamps from the keys of a foreign typewriter. Lovely Christmas line – but another nasty type of fraud!

Complaints

Strangely, very few boot punters complain about the stuff they buy when you consider how much of it is dodgy. The buyers of Peter's 'gold' chains probably still have them, blissfully unaware of the phoney hallmarks. They probably wouldn't know a real mark from fake. Sonia's bedding punters recommend her wares to others, 'So cheap for that brand'. You see, they've never owned quality, only seen the name and price they can't afford.

I'm not so sure about 'Young Del's' cars – but that's not boot gear, is it? Poor punters are used to the rough end of the stick and have low expectations. As long as it works for a few weeks and they've got something with a glam label stuck on they're happy. Incredible, init?

Chapter 8
Big Deal

Once they have discovered the easy money from basic booting, avoiding the 'pirate trap' and the folly of two-bob operators, pro booters naturally become more ambitious.

I mentioned some of the bigger types of dealing earlier on as we familiarised ourselves with the trade. So now's the time to look seriously at the bigger deals. But careful now – the bigger the deal, the bigger the risk! Be sure you are ready. Get comfortable and confident in your trade before you start mixing with the big boys.

House Clearing

One way of moving up a step without too much risk is house clearances. This was once the territory of the secondhand shop operator but there's nothing to stop the developing booter trying his or her luck at the game. The main requirements are a bit of an 'eye', a transit or similar type van or large trailer, a heart of stone and a skin like a rhino.

The basic picture is this. You put an ad in paper classifieds under 'Goods Wanted', thus:

HOUSE CLEARANCES
HOUSES CLEARED. DECEASED'S EFFECTS, UNWANTED FURNITURE
APPLIANCES ETC. REMOVED CLEANLY AND DISCREETLY
BEST PRICES PAID IN CASH. ALL GOODS WANTED
TELEPHONE 12345

There are a number of 'truth economies' in the advert – but that's advertising!

ALL GOODS WANTED means – only if they will fetch good money. Otherwise you will have to ask a fee to cart away the load of tot (useless rubbish) you have called to inspect.

BEST PRICES means – as little as you can get away with. The best price for anything to a dealer is nothing. Even better is being paid to take away stuff that can be sold. That is the real winner but it takes a clever operator who really knows the biz.

As booters, we know that almost anything can be sold. But making a profit from two 1950s wardrobes and a moth-eaten three piece suite, AFTER their removal costs, is beyond even the best in the trade. You are entitled to say 'thanks for the chance, but no thanks' – and quite a few calls end in that. You have to be FIRM. Solid as the Rock of Gibraltar cos the client is desperate to shift the trash that is preventing the sale of the house.

This is the usual scenario. Client's old mum or whatever has gone beyond. Client inherits house furnished with the sad chattels of the autumn years. The family has taken what's worth having and needs to clear the 'drum' (house) so it can be sold. 'There's nothing like tatty furniture hanging around to kill a sale', says the estate agent. 'Get a clearance man in'.

How You Do It

If it's junk and they admit it, ask for a fee to clear it – or no deal.

Weed out anything that might sell. Dump the rest at 'tip' (Local Authority rubbish dump, sometimes called 'civic amenity'). Beware of 'hawks', see chapter 4.

Make sure your fee covers transport costs, tip fees (traders have to pay – visit regular and you will be sussed as trade) and a profit.

If it's mostly junk with a few good bits, still try as above and make better profit. If they want cash, say thanks and leave. You might frighten them into a deal.

What you are looking for is a decent load with some tasty bits that will fetch good dough – not too much tip stuff – and paying out a few pounds at worst. Still, remember your costs! You do need experience but a few months' booting will give you that. House clearers have earned thousands from a load they paid £20 for.

Charlie has been clearing houses for years. Here are his tips for clearers.

Charlie's Tale

Three generations of my family have been dealers. I can sum up what's in a house just by looking at the outside but I always take a quick look in, just in case.

Newish property has little to offer. These are mortgage snatch-backs or broken marriages. Either way, they will be looking for more dough than I'm prepared to pay. They've usually sold the best through the paper, want the crap cleared and have no money to pay for that service.

The best hit is an oldish place in a still respectable part of town. Over the years, old folk accumulate bits that become valuable without them knowing it.

As I go round the drum, I take a quick look in drawers and cupboards. The client thinks I am valuing the furniture, but actually I'm looking for nice little bits. It's just a quick in and out of the drawer, a look at the joinery work – but my 'eye' is scanning the contents for a piece that, to me, stands out like a boil on a kid's bum.

If there's stuff worth having I make a reasonable trade offer for the furniture and the good bits are bonus. We clear immediately. Plenty of times a client will leave something good just to get you to make a deal, then when you come to collect the next day the good bit's gone!

Our deal is we take everything – house, shed, garage, cellar, the lot. If they want me to take only part, I say 'clear what you want, then I'll come back and reassess the situation'. That way there's no arguments about what was or was not on offer.

If people get difficult, it's usually cos there's something to hide. The will ain't been read yet or they're getting in before the rest of the family arrive. You just leave and let some other mug get caught up in the mess. There's plenty of good biz without that kind of aggro.

Do ask for proof of right to sell. Many a dealer has been caught loading up the goods that a burglar, pretending to own the house, sold to him while the householders were away. Always suspect a house that looks as if it is still in occupation with a lot of personal stuff around. An honest seller won't mind you asking the reason for sale. I've known a lodger sell a whole house full and do an 'offman' (run for it) while the dealer's loading up the gear. This situation takes a lot of explaining at the police station – particularly if the lodger has vanished.

You keep your offers low and be ready to deal with a lot of emotion when stuff is deceased property. It's not a game for the soft hearted. You need to be a bit diplomatic, but businesslike at the same time – what my dad used to call soft soaping them. The clients should feel you've done them a favour as the van pulls away, full up.

A clearance should be quick and neat, no fuss. I have strong lads who I pay cash in hand to shift stuff. I try to get an idea of the bulk on the phone so when we arrive we are ready to shift it. The boys are experienced removal hands and do the job without mess or noise. It all helps to impress the client.

Remember you are handling the last links with a dear departed. So be tactful – no silly jokes or tomfoolery. It isn't moving day or a happy occasion. Sometimes there's even a 'drink' (tip) for the crew when the thing goes well.

On a big clear, EVERYTHING goes back to my premises. The furniture is moved, full up if possible. That way you sort through its contents privately. You'd be amazed at the bits of gold and what not that turn up at the bottom of boxes and in the backs of chairs.

You never let the client see you search through stuff. Just get out of the drum fast as possible. Boxes from cellars and attics can be full of good stuff. Undisturbed boxes and cases are the best. You can tell if the client's been through them with a fine toothcomb by the fingerprints in the dust. I price the job accordingly but still find little treasures – that's where the 'eye' counts.

So, summing up, it's Experience, Diplomacy, and Firmness. It's hard work and often very dirty. But it can be an excellent living if you buy and sell well.

———

A very good account of the clearance biz, there. Our thanks to Charlie for that info on a very secretive trade. Our next big deal is the auction houses.

Auctions

They fall into four distinct categories. CLASS, GENERAL, JUNK AND PHONEY.

CLASS. The big time 'rooms', as they are called, selling genuine antiques of high value. Your dealings with them will only be when you find something of real worth and they sell it for you. They will give opinion and valuation without embarrassing you; but don't waste their time with an endless stream of trivial rubbish.

GENERAL. Every town has its auction rooms. Check the Yellow Pages for details. Go to a few sales and watch what goes on. You will learn a lot about prices and start to develop an 'eye'. Get catalogues from sales to keep as reference. Ask to be put on their mailing list as a dealer.

An auctioneer is a very good contact. Always keep your dealings with auctioneers absolutely straight and truthful for they are valuable allies and powerful friends. They know the requirements of your business. An auction house is one place that you can take a cheque from with confidence.

It is through a general sale that most of your better finds will be sold. If something is really valuable, an auctioneer will tell you so; and will advise on its sale.

JUNK. Most general auctioneers hold regular sales of low-value goods. These are very useful for buying and selling. Again, I would advise you to attend a few sales just to watch before you start buying. Put in a few bits that are too good for boots and see how you do. It's all trial and error until you learn what's what.

There are lots of junk-only auctions, particularly in rural areas. They are well worth a visit, most taking place on week days. Good boot stuff is often bought at nothing prices. Big boxes of useful stuff for as little as £1.50 – lots of dealers after these. Informal atmosphere and good contacts.

Many 'off the course' (private) deals take place at small auctions. They are good places to get known as a dealer.

PHONEY. Not exactly illegal but a bit of a con. You see them in the papers like this: 'One day auction/sale of frustrated export/bankrupt stock'.

The lines offered are oriental rugs, household goods, paintings and prints – that kind of stuff. These events are in a hall hired for the day.

The purchaser usually pays more than shop prices for second quality stuff. It's for mug punters. Dealers don't go. Nor should you. But see one without buying – just to learn what goes on.

Commercial Auctions

Some genuine auction rooms have a commercial department that deals solely with the stock of bankrupt or liquidated companies. Goods from the Official Receiver, bailiffs, or simply stock that needs quick disposal for cash flow. The goods may be slightly damaged or a miss-make (anything that makes disposal through normal channels difficult). If you are on the mailing list, you will get a catalogue for the sale and be able to consider what might be worth buying well before it goes on view.

Even so, ALWAYS view before you bid. It can save you a lot of money and pain. A chum of mine once bid for 3,000 kitchen clocks without viewing them. He got them for £200 – a bargain he thought. They were very nice clocks and they were all working too! Problem was they went backwards! It took him 2 years to get rid of them at £100.

At these sort of auctions you buy 'job' (big lots at low prices). There are bargains but you need storage and the confidence that your profit will justify tying money up for a time.

Again, proceed cautiously. Buy once and see how you do. Watch other dealers at the sale working on calculators the margin of profit as the bidding rises. Never be panicked into buying for this won't be the last sale on earth. Clever and cautious buyers win. Allow yourself time to get clever. DON'T spend what you can't afford, hoping for a quick profit. Think what you could LOSE rather than what you could gain.

Job Dealers

These guys are dealers' dealers. They are big-time operators, working with hefty capital and access to large overdraft facilities at the bank. They often buy in millions and have vast storage for their stock – goods, which for a number of legitimate reasons, cannot be sold through normal channels.

Though you will find them in the phone book, they don't advertise except in trade papers and are not interested in dealing retail with the general public.

Jobbers sometimes have shops through which they clear lines of a general nature at heavily discounted prices. Many of what have become known as 'market shops' are in fact owned by a jobber with a manager in charge.

A jobber works on a vast network of contacts and does massive amounts of business by phone, often selling goods by 'gentlemen's agreement' before he has taken delivery. Sometimes the goods go from point of purchase to buyer without ever passing through the jobber's hands, except on paper.

Many market traders get their stock from job dealers. To deal job you have to be prepared to buy bulk, to know how to haggle like a Gypsy, and to pay cash. The stuff can be unbelievably cheap – as little as 2 or 3 per cent of retail price – but there is always something not quite right with it. That's why it came to the jobber to clear.

Really, you need to be a trader (market stall holder) as opposed to a booter, to take advantage of a jobber's services. But many full traders started in booting and moved into trading.

In trading, you tend to stick to one line – like china and glass or linen goods or clothing, all new – rather than the mix that is the booter's stock. Jobber's stock appears at auctions; and this is perhaps where the booter may be better placed to buy stuff that may not suit the 'one-line' trader.

You need to be well 'up the ladder' (advanced in the biz) before you start to deal direct with jobbers. When you've got going properly in boots, go and see a jobber and ask if he has lines that might suit you. Although very busy, a jobber will always be interested to make a new contact. A few minutes is all it needs – a quick chat. Keep it brief and leave your phone number. You will then be on his list and get offered stuff he thinks might suit.

The jobber is probably the most efficient business man you will ever meet, but he can't stand time-wasters. Many booters have made the transition to traders through a jobber's help.

If you come across a vast deal looking for a buyer, pass the info to your jobber. He will not forget the 'introduction' as it's called and will look favourably upon you by perhaps giving you first option on a good deal of which he has a limited supply.

The more money you spend with jobbers the more stuff you will be offered at even less money. Their supply of goods is endless. DON'T get carried away. Know your limits. Be able to say NO politely, but always thank him for the offer. Respect is important to jobbers and they respect straight talkers. Bullshit gets you nowhere with them.

Eccentrics

They abound. Militaria freaks, collectors of all that's weird and wonderful, specialists in every field – clocks, barber's equipment, costumes, stamps, cigarette cards, autographs, trains, transport. Name anything and someone will specialise.

Many are fanatics who live for their hobby, which for some becomes a business. They often deal world-wide and hunt for items that fetch hundreds or even thousands of pounds.

You gather their names and phone numbers. When a good piece comes in, get in touch. It can be good biz. Most haunt the boots regularly and so save you the cost of a call.

Collectors will pay the earth and go without food for a missing item in a collection (see chapter 10).

Contacts are important – for certain things never go on display. All the foreign coins and stamps I get go to one buyer. O.K., so sometimes I might sell a bit too cheap; but I haven't got time to value every stamp and coin that comes through. If it looks a bit unusual, a quick check in the catalogues and guides I keep is enough. I then ring my contact. He will also take all the run-of-the-mill stuff in bulk from me for a few pounds to retain my interest in offering him the better stuff.

It's swings and roundabouts, you see. Quick turnover and profit. You don't want schoolboys poring over a box of stamps or coins for a few pence and pinching most of them. They just make the flash untidy. Stamps blow away or get damaged – bulk 'em out.

Guvvy Stuff

This is the trade term for what was once called 'Military Surplus' – all the stuff that the Government thought it needed and bought with our taxes, then found out it never needed at all and sold off at a fraction of its price.

The stuff can be anything from an office desk to a fire engine. Vast sales of guvvy are held at military bases and Government warehouses. They can comprise as many as 10,000 lots and be a mixture of military and/or civil service equipment and supplies.

Much of it has never been used, is still packaged, and is sold by auction or tender (highest bid by letter, a sort of blind auction). Bids can be so low as to be a joke, but 'everything must go', as they say, so the Government can buy some more!

At the end of the war in 1946, dealers made fortunes from guvvy. Now, as the 'cold war' ends, millions more tons of guvvy are being sold off. If you need a commercial vehicle or a car 'one owner, hardly used', a guvvy sale is a must. Your new transport will come with loads of spares and extra bits, and will cost you the price of a new bicycle in the shops.

The sales are advertised in trade papers. Also, the larger commercial auctioneers, who organize sales for the guv, send out catalogues.

Last year, I went with a dealing mate to one in Plymouth. He bought a large two-year old van with just 8,000 miles on the clock. It came with a brand new spare engine, ten new spare tyres, a kit of tools large enough to open a garage and 5 cases containing unopened tins of grease. Price for that lot? £320! At the same sale, two virtually new estate cars were knocked down at £800 each – a tenth of their value. True, they were in military paintwork, but what does a cheap respray cost? You could hand-paint it if it's just for work.

I bought 80 of those insulated 'picnic boxes'- you know, the big ones with handles? I think they'd been used for medical gear. A drop of thinners got the guv stencils off. A quick wash and they sold easy at a fiver each. Buying price? £10 the lot! You sort of get one back on the Chancellor at these do's.

Made to Sell

This is the term for novelty stuff, sold bulk, that usually comes from more obscure parts of the Far East or Eastern Europe. The stuff is utter trash and has no use other than for selling to mugs at coastal or 'event-type' do's, where folk impulse buy for tiny prices and usually lose or break the stuff before they get home.

It also includes the sort of stuff that is given as 'prizes' at fairground stalls and bingos. It's called M.T.S. stock cos that's all it's good for – just selling and amusing feeble minds. At Christmas, a booter can do well from a 'lucky dip' at the side of the flash. No one complains at 20p a go, or you can sell '10 for a pound' tree trimmings. Cost? £10 a thousand or so, a bit more for pot and glass stuff.

Seaside traders buy this stuff a thousand pounds worth at a time... AND... and I do like to be beside the seaside. A boot pitch at a seaside town in summer still costs only £10 or so. Seafront traders pay £100 a day or more. Ipso facto – well I don't have to tell you by now, do I?

Chapter 9
A Genuine Antique

Just how many genuine antiques are left in Britain is anyone's guess. Good items continue to turn up and the boot trade discovers its fair share.

The Great Myth

Just recently a painting bought at a booter in Bristol for £2 realized £67,000 at auction. Though finds of this kind are rare, they give rise to folk-tales that every boot sale contains dozens of similar bargains that will make your fortune.

This Great Myth, as it's called in the trade, is given credence by television shows like Antiques Roadshow and – with tongue in cheek – Lovejoy, the loveable rogue dealer played superbly by Ian McShane (any chance of a 'walk on', guv?) who seems to stumble on some priceless relic every week.

It's all great entertainment. But what the gullible public fails to realize is that for every real 'find', the average dealer shifts TONS of rubbish. It's nothing unusual to sell for £10 what you got for a few pence, but the fabulous discovery is a rare event.

Of course, the 'myth' is cultivated by the trade. That's what bumps up the price of junk, which just MIGHT be a find if you get the right mug 'on the string' (encouraged to let their imagination fool them). The 'ant' trade is a minefield of traps for the unwary – with many different facets. Here are the most common divisions of 'ant'.

Exporting

For years now smart dealers have been shipping container loads of 'old stuff' to America, Canada, and more recently to Australia.

The demand for this mix of genuine antiques, 'talking pieces' (interesting or odd things) and pure junk, comes mostly from designer types who 'decorate' homes in the sense of themes in furniture and accessories rather than wallpaper and paint.

Much of the stuff exported for this trade has its value in appearance rather than in its worth as an antique – though at the better end, quite a few real antiques go down this road.

Along with them goes a good deal more stuff posing as antiques that were out-and-out fakes made just for the 'expo' trade. When fashion and money-to-waste enter the shop, morals exit very quickly.

Antique forgers are nothing new. In Victorian times, copies of classic pieces of furniture were all the rage. Millions were made and, having now acquired the dignity of age, often pass as the real thing to those with less knowledge than dough. The 'Vicky' fakers were expert craftsmen. They turned out superb copies that can easily deceive all but the real professional 'eye'.

Though it has reduced, the trade in bulk export is still busy and the boot game is a good hunting ground for exporters looking for cheap buys. Many employ permanent 'scouts' to bring in stuff from such sources. They are far too busy 'tarting up' (giving the appearance of better quality) stuff to do their own shopping.

Dealers do a lot of biz with the expo crowd. The trick is to spot the sort of stuff that catches expo trends. An expo man will often tell you what style he's looking for, especially if you have a regular supply of stuff coming through. Expo is good for clearing larger furniture, oddballs and fakes that have only 'decorative talent' (little or no antique value).

Auctions

Auctions are vital to the ant trade.

Auction houses can value items, can bring in experts and can advertise availability much wider than a shop or individual dealer. They have many contacts, including wealthy collectors, and are the only people worthy of any real trust in a trade seething with devious types. But even the best can and do make mistakes – but fortunately, not too often.

Experts

There are probably more in antiques than in any other field of human endeavour, except perhaps business advice and consultancy. When you see how many firms go bust even with 'good advice', you realise that a second opinion isn't a bad idea.

Don't let appearances fool you. Some of the best experts I've met were as poor as the proverbial church mice. It's the wealthy ones you need to watch. Nuf said?

Low Antiques

This is the dangerous ground. The stuff looks old, looks like it's worth something and has fads amongst collectors – like 'kitchenalia' (old catering equipment). But fakes and frauds are everywhere.

The Far East turns out 'repros' (reproductions) in millions from a single genuine example. Oil lamps and the like in classic Vicky styles are some. These are recognizable to a slightly skilled 'eye'. But with a little extra work, the repro becomes an original and the trap is set.

India is the big producer of the 'brassy' stuff that is now flooding the market. Repros get more and more convincing. China and jade are being faked to fool the unwary and then sold as the real thing to new ant enthusiasts. Many idiots buy as the real thing even when the 'Made in India' stamp appears prominently on a pair of supposed Worcester vases!

Collectables

Can be ANYTHING. If you've got something odd on the flash and you know it's not worth a carrot, as we say, you put on a ticket saying 'Very Collectable'. Some twit will pay good money and start collecting them in the hope that the stuff will go up in value. Sometimes it does!

You watch your auction catalogues and various published guides for new trends in 'coll'. Most of the better newspapers carry regular features on coll, including latest trends and current values.

Pre-1939 televisions are now fetching vast sums. Old teddy bears have done so for several years. Comics and old children's books steadily rise in price. Any number can win. Catch a trend early, or START one, and you can make a fortune.

Limited Editions

This is another dubious field spawned by the fascination for ant and coll.

Smart manufacturers turn out special lines of coins, plates, dolls, books, anything you like. The idea is you 'invest' in the set, sit back and wait for it to rise in price. It might in about 200 years. But then so will anything, if it survives – and it will cost a lot less than these 'investments'.

Sooner or later someone will produce a 'limited edition' (ten million copies) of a set of cracked chamber pots, depicting scenes of famous car smashes on the M25 and thousands will buy it on the advertiser's 'credit card hot line'. Oh Gawd! I hope I ain't given away a good idea.

Art

You must be a real expert to deal and make money in art. In modern art, you just need to have a lot of money to deal. If you like a picture and it's got an oldish frame and it's dead cheap – like nothing – have it. Someone will give you a profit.

Art is something where you have to have real knowledge. I can't teach you that here. Learn the difference between a print, an oil and a water-colour – that alone puts you in a knowledge bracket of less than 10 per cent of the population. Learn who the 100 most famous painters in the world are/were and you've got it down to 5 per cent. Know who the 100 most famous English painters are or were and you're in less than 1 per cent. Be able to recognize the work of those painters and you are, believe it or not, an expert.

That will be £500 please. Well? You could pay that much for a course and learn far less!

Books

This is another highly specialized field. There are, and have been, far more writers than artists – so there's even more to know.

Modern paperback novels are a steady earner for the booter. Current 'papers' can cost up to £10. Hardbacks up to £20 or more. A few months old book from a popular writer, in excellent condition, will achieve about a third of its original price. But 'antiquarian books', as the trade calls them, are another thing altogether. So here's a rough guide:

Bibles

This is the world's best seller!

Later than 1850 – worth very little unless spectacular binding.
1800 to 1850 – not a lot, but can 'fetch' at auction.
Pre-1800 – worth a book dealer's opinion.
Pre-1700 – well worth a book dealer's opinion. Should do well, but not fantastic unless something 'special'.

General Books Pre-1900

Take these to a book dealer in bulk. One in a hundred is worth a few quid.

General Books Pre-1800

All worth something. Dealer again for a few quid each – or see an auctioneer.

Older than Above

Get an auctioneer's valuation – for dealers' greed will now overcome their ethics.

Maps and Geographic Books of any Age

This is a big collector field. Proceed as above; but don't take the first offer.

Old Comics, 'School' Books, 50s/60s Annuals, Rupert etc.

These are all collectables. Take them to the many specialist shops.

Mills and Boon

20 pence each.

Art Folios, Books of Paintings

Wrap in clear plastic and display UNPRICED. Ask what you think is a ridiculously high price. Some twit will pay it.

That is the end of the literary course. The rest you learn from experience. It takes 20 years to become a book expert and there are no short cuts. When you've handled as many secondhand books as I have, you'll stop worrying that you might have lost on the odd one.

Very valuable books are rarer than very valuable antiques – the vast majority are worth whatever you can get. So don't waste too much time on them.

Classic Cars

At present, this is an all but collapsed market and vast losses have been reported. In the real classics, it was always a field for fanatics with money to lose. Now they've lost it, some are wishing they hadn't. The smart money got out five years ago. DON'T BOTHER.

Wine

If you can afford to go to classic wine sales AND buy, I can't imagine why you bought this book. Still, that's your biz. But you've got more money than I have – or far more patience to wait for a profit.

Cheers. This is one field I know absolutely nothing about, being almost teetotal. Sorry!

Real Antiques

'I thought we'd never get there', says you. Well, when you walk across a field, you look for where the cow pats are, not the grass, don't you?

Spotting a real antique needs good knowledge or the 'eye'. The knowledge? Well, we're talking about 10,000 years of stuff from all over the world – so it may take you a bit longer than the art course you just did.

What do you mean, what art course? The one you gave me that monkey's worth of dud cheque for. You're getting quite good you know and we're only two-thirds of the way through the book!

NO ONE is expert on all antiques. You can have a good overall idea or you can specialize in a particular field. The last 400 years is where the bulk comes from. The chances of you finding a bit of early Mayan gold or a new Dead Sea Scroll are just about zilch minus – so don't even worry about it. Even a knowledge of the last 200 years will stand you in good stead. But that will take years if all you know is what they keep at M.F.I.

What you need is the 'eye'. 'YES' says you 'So you've said umpteen times, but what is it?' I've held this bit back until now to get you keen – cos this is probably the most valuable bit of gen in the whole book. It will earn you more dough than anything else. But it takes a little while to explain. So brew another cuppa, find a nice quiet spot and discover the secret of overnight – well almost – expertise!

The Eye

This is an instinctive feel for antique items – the ability of not so much experts, who are often blinded by accumulated knowledge, but of those who let their senses guide them.

Totally illiterate folk, with no idea whatsoever of history, can have the eye. It's not inherited or magic or witchcraft. It needs no education but just the ability to use the senses – hearing, seeing, smelling, taste and touch, plus that sixth sense, gut feeling.

Familiarity

Once you have been booting for a few months, you will have seen an awful lot of stuff. If you have listened to the words of sage advice herein, you will have attended auctions, hoarded sale catalogues, obtained antique and collectors' guides and probably developed a lot of knowledge without even knowing it.

Much of that knowledge you think you don't remember. But you DO. Locked away in your mind are all the facts, things and pictures you have seen. All together, they are giving you more familiarity with stuff every day.

If you were 'put under' by a hypnotist, you would be able to recall every single thing you've handled, seen, read or heard. You may not know it, but every time you pick up a new thing the computer in your brain will cross-reference it in a fraction of a second to answer your silent question 'What's this?' All you have to do is let your senses do the work. Stop trying to think consciously and let your subconscious take over.

'Now I've heard it all' says you. 'This is a load of goolies'. IS it? Even experts in antiques acknowledge the 'eye' – that they know more from just handling stuff than they ever learned at college or from books. They know that an antique can be 'divined' by the senses just as much as looked up in books. In fact those who spot the fakes do so more from the senses than from info in books.

First you have to want to know. Then your brain receives an instruction without your consciously knowing it. The brain sets up a programme for the job and the incoming facts and pictures go into that programme, ready for you to use if you know how.

The Eye in Practice

Right. A hypothetical case. You have done a little house clearance and have got the gear back to your lair. Amongst the stuff is a box, about shoe-box size. Let's let the eye do its job.

Does it look old?

What colour is it?

How dirty is it? Just dirty, or has it built up a 'patina' (a kind of shell of dirt that has transparent depth)?

What's it made of?

Are there any marks, writing or labels on the outside? Use a magnifying glass.

What sort of fittings, if any, are attached? Apply questions as above.

What's its shape? Does it look like something you've seen before?

What was that thing? Age? Period?

What's the inside like – lining? cloth? paper? any fittings?

What does it smell of? Are there any substances or traces of substances?

Does it look well-made? Good or very small joints? Are they hard to see?

Does it feel nice to handle?

Is it trying to tell you something? This is a question to your own subcon.

What do I think this might be?

Is it worth a second opinion?

Analysis

The box looks old. It is made of wood, very dark but a bit shiny. It is plain but has a small lock. The fittings are a bit thick for their size. Under the magnifier, an initial and a name are almost visible, clogged with a skin of old polish and dirt, on the bottom.

It has four small feet. Inside there is nothing; but there are marks as if something was slid in and out. There is a smell of something – not just an old musty smell, but something sharper and more lingering.

It looks like an old-fashioned coffin, but very small. It's joined together but there is no way of seeing how it's joined – not even in the places where the sides come together. It fits perfectly and is very well-made. It feels right to handle, sort of balanced.

It's for keeping something in – what? What made those marks? What is it? What's it trying to tell me?

Tea! That smell – yes, it's tea. The shape inside and the marks? – there were two things that went inside, fitted in.

Wait a minute, those other two metal boxes in the case? – yes, they fit in and match the marks! There's still a tiny bit of tea in this one! It looks a really nice thing.

It's a Georgian tea caddy. You've now checked your reference books. Take it to your auctioneer. Yes, it will fetch about £250.

Don't believe it? That happened to me the second time I did a house-clearance; and I knew sweet Fanny Adams about antiques – just what I'd been told about the eye.

You see old caddys on two-bob booters' stalls. They think it's just 'some old box'. 'How much?' 'Oh, couple of quid, chief?' 'Give you a pound' 'O.K.' Easy init? Even without the internal tea boxes, you're talking fifty to a hundred quid today.

If you practise and let your eye develop, you can run your hand over a piece and get an instinctive 'feel' for its value. It's not magic. Your mind is doing the job you've asked it to do.

You'll suss the smell of cement and fag-ash used to produce the 'old' dust of antiquity. You'll know the feel of real old wood against modern, doctored with paints and vinegar to look old. You'll register the marks of the chain used to 'age' a piece. You can never really fake a hundred years of use without leaving a tiny clue somewhere. To the eye, it stands out like an ink blot on a white bedsheet.

Woolworths or Worcester

There are a million tricks like the above to fake an ant but no one tries to make a real 'un look fake. The real thing shines out like a diamond in a dung heap.

Use your eye. And also while you are looking, if there's a seller involved, glance up suddenly at his eye. If you are starting to suss the phoney, his look – caught unawares – will tell you the rest. If he's looking away, at nothing in particular, it's a fake. He don't want to catch your eye cos his mind's saying 'Don't suss it'. You'll learn by experience.

Look for the maker's mark on china. All good pot has marks and you can get quite good small books to guide you. If there is the mark of a good maker, dig your thumb nail into the bottom. If it leaves an impression the piece has been 'bottomed'. That means a plain fake or repro has been given a maker's mark and then painted over with a clear polymer which looks just like glaze but is not quite so hard. You can't mark real glaze except with really hard metal or a diamond.

Silver and Gold

This must have real hallmarks. There are not many and they don't take long to learn. You will find illustrations in any small encyclopaedia or almanac.

Always carry a jeweller's glass. Even small pieces of jewellery will have marks somewhere – but these will be near invisible to the naked eye. No mark – base metal! And no jeweller mounts good stones in base metal.

Costume or paste jewellery can be worth money but needs real ability to know it. Here the eye may be defeated by collectable value. It's something you have to learn the hard way. Well, you can't have it all easy can you?

Let's get something straight. I can't teach you success. I can't even teach you all the pitfalls. What I can do is help you avoid the pratt falls that the two-bob booters make. The eye takes time to learn – but you can make good money from bread-and-butter booting while you are learning.

I look back, as you will, to things which I should have done much better on – things that someone else made more dough from than I did. But I still made a profit and learned from experience. If I had titled this book 'Become an Antiques Expert in Seven Days', you wouldn't have bought it, would you? Of course not because you know that's nonsense. What I am saying is that you can become knowledgeable, just as most dealers did, by experience and a little guidance from others in the trade itself – no more than that.

No one, except a complete idiot, wants to see the physical remnants of our past end up on a council tip. They are part of history and should be preserved. If this was a silly idea, there would be no museums and no antiques trade.

Money is a motivating factor; but so also is a love for the things themselves. The more you deal in antique items the more you will begin to understand this enthusiasm for their preservation. Who knows? You might just end up as an antique dealer. It can creep up on you. All you have to do is want it to happen and keep shifting the stuff!

Sizing

'Sizing' stands for sizing 'em up. No section on ant is complete without this valuable skill which I promised to give you in chapter 6. I think you're ready for it now, before we do the Sales Finishing Course in the next chapter.

When you sell ant or supposed ant, you set the price to the PUNTER not the item – that's why ant and coll don't have price labels. Trade knows the value and will haggle for the RIGHT price. BUT there's an awful lot of mugs out there who will pay too much if you handle them right. So you size 'em up.

Clothes and speech give a lot away, even today. Wealthy people try to look poor at a boot sale but forget little things like quality frames on eye-glasses, manicured nails, class leather shoes, styles of speech. While the punter is examining ant or coll, YOU examine him or her.

The man in that old, grubby mac is wearing expensive leather brogue shoes. He gets out his specs – gold, half-bifocal. The greasy cap doesn't fool us. Up goes the price. He dressed down to try to buy reasonable – but his disguise wasn't good enough!

The lady looks like every other housewife – but that head scarf is Italian silk. And the handbag? That's the Cartier logo isn't it? She thought we wouldn't notice cos of the C & A coat. But we deal in gear. IT'S OUR JOB TO NOTICE.

She asks 'How much do you want for this?' Dead give-away! Diction's too good. An 'oik' (poor person) would have said 'How much is this?' or 'What's the price of this'. That 'do you' and not using the word 'price' divides her from the oiks – like Moses divided the Red Sea. The £25 touch jumps to £50.

Takes a while to learn sizing; but six months on a boot stall and you will guess the income of 99 out of 100 punters. Just keep your eyes and ears open and learn to recognise quality clothing and accessories.

Right, let's learn how to catch every last little punter-fish in the 'Super Sales Course' in the next chapter.

Chapter 10
There's No Business Like ...

'Don't put your daughter on the stage' wrote Noel Coward. This is probably good advice when you see the number of actors out of work, or 'resting' as their profession calls it. Quite a few 'resting' actors do boot sales. They take money; but few are in the major league of earners in the game and this puzzles me.

An expression often heard amongst booters is 'there's no business like Schmo business'. This refers to the 'Joe Schmo' or mug-type punter, who will believe the most absurd sales talk. That's today's lesson, students.

How to Sell

If you've ever fancied a 'life on the boards' (acting), booting is a good second choice when you find how badly acting pays. There are probably half a million actors in Britain alone and few of them will ever achieve any kind of stardom. Most have other jobs for they would starve to death on what they earn from acting. Having seen some of their 'performances' at boot sales, I can understand why.

Selling is a form of acting, or entertaining if you like. Your gaff is a kind of mini stage and the punters are the audience who react very well if you entertain them. I don't mean put on a funny hat and give them a burst on the old banjo. But it is important to make the process of parting with money an interesting experience.

You do need to be a bit extrovert to stand behind a stall and deal with the public; and there are many links between street markets and the world of entertainment – particularly if you go back to the old Music Hall days. Gus Elland was billed as the 'Coster Comic' eighty years ago when many of the 'Halls' were adjacent to or right in street markets. The costers or street traders often comprised a large proportion of the audience. They loved songs about their trade and its associated lifestyle.

The Halls were rough and ready – as boisterous as the street markets around them. They reflected the garish and, some might say, tasteless but colourful, 'show biz' style of street trading. The stall-holder puts on a show and, in this, has much in common with the actor on his stage.

So why don't actors do well as stall-holders? I've no doubt that the great Music Hall and Variety Theatre stars like Marie Lloyd, Max Miller or Gus Elland would have made wonderfully successful booters. Nell Gwyn sold oranges before she got well-connected with Royalty and took to a stage career. But that was all a long while ago – and acting has changed since those days.

Today's young actors are serious beings, often with a long drama school training behind them. Theirs is a serious profession and the quality of today's film and television drama requires a more scientific approach than the knock-about spontaneity of the Music Hall. Off-stage they tend to be studious, almost apologetic in their approach to life – not the require-ments for stall trade, which is still the old 'keep em laughing' business. The Carry-On crew is more in the stall holder's style.

I did once try to help an actor improve his sales technique. He had good stock, and there was a lot of interest from the punters in his flash, but he just wasn't turning the goods. He wasn't 'selling' – just letting the punters lead the sale.

In a quiet moment (he was set up next to me), I got in the tea and bacon butties and had a chat. I suggested that, instead of letting the pun-ters lead, he should play his role as a 'part', literally acting the role of a market stall holder. 'But', said my new thespian chum, 'I'd need a script and a rehearsal and a director to show me what to do'.

Being a bloody know-all, I asked 'What about that 'method acting' lark, where you become the person you're playing all the time until the show's over?'

'Well, you need to study the person in real life, if possible, and copy their movements and speech. It takes ages, months', said Ken the actor.

Me: 'You don't think I'm like this all the time, do you? I'm acting with the punters, giving them a laugh and making it fun. I'm being what they expect – a bit Jack the Lad, bright and breezy, entertaining them. I'm totally different when the sale's over'.

Our Ken was dumbstruck. He joined me and a few chums at a pub for a pint of shandy after the do (I don't drink much – like to keep the old noddy clear in case a deal comes up). He was amazed how we'd all changed, become 'normal' after the sale.

'You should be in acting' says Ken. 'I appreciate the compliment, but £50 a day once in a blue moon?', says I. 'No thanks, Ken, but you should see me play the gallery when we have a charity sale and all dress up for fun. My Dolly Parton impersonation's legendary!'

Ken's acting career is developing, I saw him on telly a few weeks back, playing a villain in a cops-and-robbers thing. Very good he was too. Nothing like the polite, rather shy young man who booted next to me that day. Good luck to him; but it would take a lot of work to make a dealer of him. Maybe with Steven Spielberg directing?

Selling

Right back in chapter 2, I said 'sell yourself'. Selling is an art and a form of entertaining. Now we'll do the advanced course for the those who have got the hang of the basics and want to learn real selling.

A wry quip used between booters on slow days is 'have you tried selling it?' There's a lot more than just an ironic joke here. Some booters never really sell. They wonder why the goods aren't sold and yet they are giving out the message 'I don't want to sell' without noticing it. We're talking 'body language' here.

Body Language

This consists of movements, poses or unspoken signals that send messages to others. Here's an example.

Booter stalls-out, prices up stuff, checks float of change, gets cup of tea, leans back against car boot, folds arms and looks down at stock. What's he saying?

Right! He's saying I'm ignoring you (punter) and I'm having my tea. My arms are folded cos I want to put a barrier between you and me. I dare you to disturb me by asking a question that might lead to a sale. I am not really interested in doing business.

Second example.

Same set-up but booter stands behind flash, looks up and down the walkway, hands behind back, smiles at passers by, saying 'good morning' or 'lovely day' (even if it's lousy) to those who look at him or at the flash. What's he saying?

Right! I'm open and ready for biz. I've nothing to hide. I am nice to deal with. Please come and look at my stock. I will answer questions without obligation. I am interested in you.

Which booter will make a sale?

Those who said number one should immediately seek medical help.

Those who said number two are a great relief to me.

Creating Customers

'A smile is worth a million dollars' said Mr Singer, whose sewing-machine empire relied on salesmen. 'If there's no demand, create one' was another of his favourites.

How do you create a demand, create a customer? Smile and say hello, make a friendly joke, admire their dog, their tee shirt, anything. Create contact and you create a customer.

If you hate the punters, they will hate you. Do you give money to people you hate if you don't have to? Punters don't have to buy – it's your job to make them want to. Ignore the punters and they will ignore you.

The world is full of lonely people, as Paul McCartney wrote in Eleanor Rigby. Make them feel wanted and they will want to know you. Don't put out signals that say 'CLOSED FOR EVERYTHING'. Put out a flag that says 'CUSTOMERS WANTED, NO EXPERIENCE NECESSARY'. A lot of folk will apply for the job.

Playing the Crowd

Jack, one of the 'lean back against the boot' types, says I am a 'nutter'. He doesn't like me because I 'play the crowd' – which he finds embarrassing and undignified.

He also doesn't like me because I take a lot more money than him. He hates 'that flash motor', 'them poncy clothes', 'all that rabbit' (sales talk). If he comes on to the ven and sees me stalling-out, he'll pitch as far away as possible, even if that means pitching a dog position.

Harold, on the other hand, will always pitch next door if he sees a vacant spot beside me. We're great 'old mates' but he'll always ask, as ven manners require, if it's O.K. to pitch next door. Jack will just pull in and ignore his neighbour. Starting to get the pic?

Harold reckons I'm a 'draw' (a seller who tends to encourage a crowd) and he always does better beside me. He avoids pitching next to Jack. It's all a bit petty really but makes sense. To Jack, everyone is 'mate', 'pal' or 'darlin', said with a hint of a sneer (what I call 'service with a snarl'). I call people 'sir' and 'madame', emphasizing the 'e'. I'm no gigolo – the wife will confirm that – it just makes me different and a bit more interesting. That's 'playing the crowd'.

Acting the Part

You 'play-act', have a little routine to make them laugh. It's all rehearsed. Harold and I will pretend to be in fierce competition with each other – 'Ooh, you don't want to get it from him, you never know where it's been', and such like. It's all done with a smile and the punters love it. The jokes are as old as the hills; but it's the old 'uns that's the good 'uns.

Betty and Dick are a great team. Betty will pretend to be furious with Dick for asking too low a price for something. Sometimes the punter, completely fooled, will offer to pay more rather than cause a rift between these two. They've been booting for 15 years and swear they've never had a cross word other than in these 'amateur dramatics'.

You've got to have a bit of 'cheek'. That's what playing the crowd is about.

Spinning the Edge

When there's a good crowd at the flash but not much buying going on, you 'spin'.

'Come along ladies and gents, make an offer, you won't insult me. Professionals have tried and failed' – nice 'showy' voice for this one. 'All it needs is a bit of courage' – and as an afterthought – 'I wish I had some'.

This sort of stuff 'warms up' the crowd. A timid soul, thinking of making an offer, will rise to the challenge, encouraged by your apparent false bravado. You're clowning but it breaks the ice. If punter 'A' is seen to get a good deal, several more offers will follow. You have priced your stock to take account of offers, if you're smart.

Bouncing

You 'bounce' the impression of value off an innocent third party.

Punter 'A' wants item too cheap. He's offered £3 and you want £5. The price tab says £8. You look despairing. Pick on dozy-looking schmo type.

You. 'Here sir, you know value, don't you? This is cheap at a fiver isn't it?' They will always say 'Yes' – it's that type of question.

You. 'Right, give us your money then'. Schmo type may even get his money out!

At this point 'A' will butt in. 'Here, I want that'.

You. 'Well, all it takes is five pounds, sir'. 99 times out of a 100 you get the 'jacks' (£5) from 'A' and the crowd is highly amused.

If he stomps off, schmo might still be holding out his dough. AND, if not, some face in the crowd will have the value of the deal brought home to him and dash forward to have it. That's bouncing.

Turning a Punter

This is like turning stock. You sell the punter's bad image back to them.

Lady 'A' wants item too cheap.

You. 'Madame, if I gave you this for nothing would you take it?' 'Yes' says A, naively expecting a gift.

You. 'I thought you might. You seemed like the sort that wants something for nothing. Here, have my cheque book (feel in pocket). There's nothing in my account either'.

She's in a bad light, made to look greedy and exploiting the 'poor' seller. She might get huffy; but most expect stall-holders to be cheeky.

If she stomps off, the crowd will be on your side – seeing her as failing in an attempt to virtually steal the item. If she laughs, she will then make a better offer since you've held up a mirror and she didn't like the image she saw. That's turning.

Buying Signs

Don't think you will have to 'sell' every item – far from it. Most sales come to you with no effort; but you can kill a sale if you don't recognize the 'buying signs'.

Nervous Fawns

Couple have examined item briefly. They take a few steps back from flash and are now deep in discussion.

DON'T INTERRUPT THEM. Their actions indicate that they very much want the item at the price marked. Their discussion is probably about who's paying, or a joint purchase, or something equally personal. You must be patient and wait till they approach you.

If you interrupt them, you will frighten them off. If they ask questions, be gentle. They usually pay your marked price or require a very small reduction to meet their finances.

Can I Afford It

Similar to 'fawns'. but usually alone. Hardly examines item, then turns away and checks finances.

Again, DON'T INTERRUPT. If you disturb punters at this point, they will leave and you lose the sale.

The 'Hold-Out'

There are two kinds of 'hold out'

No1: Holds out goods in one hand, money in other. Nuf said?

No2: Holds goods but asks question. Holding the item towards you is a clear buying sign; but you must answer the question in a serious manner. Make a joke and you lose the sale.

Whenever a item is picked up and examined seriously, that's a buying sign – obvious. But what of the questions? There's a whole lot of difference between the two below:

Q.1 'Does this work, mate?'

Q.2 'This does work, doesn't it?'

Q.1 means 'I'll buy it if you reduce the price a lot.'

Q.2 means 'I'll pay your price if you assure me it's O.K.'

But they are both buying signs if the item is HELD by the punter.

If the punter asks Q.1, just pointing at the item, you have a long job on your hands. It's just an 'opening shot', not a buying sign.

Q.2 is never asked 'un-held' unless the item is too big or heavy to lift. AND EVEN THEN, the punter will be in contact with the item by holding the handle or resting a hand on top of it. It's a signal that says 'this is almost mine' a sort of reservation to purchase.

Intuition

As you get experienced, you will be able to spot a buying punter just by the way they approach the flash. Your mind will tell you the 'type' and you will have the 'stock replies' ready for their questions or actions. It's a bit like a hunter selecting the right bullet for his target or a golfer picking the right club for the shot.

The Power of Silence

This is knowing when to keep 'schtum' (your mouth shut). We've talked a lot about what to say but there are times when silence really is golden.

The top sales people in the world (they sell aeroplanes and oilfields) will tell you that their best tip in selling is to know when to STOP selling. When you have answered a punter's questions, just SHUT UP and smile pleasantly. This leaves the ball in the punter's court. They have to say something or you'll both stand there grinning till hell freezes over. There are only three things they can say:

1 'I'll have it'.
2 'Will you take (an offer)'.
3 'I'll think about it'.

Your answers:

1 'Thank you sir/madam.'
2 'I'll meet you half way' (if offer reasonable).
3 'By all means, but I can't hold it for you'. This is an opening for you to resell the item. The punter is asking you to convince them. You have begun by warning that the goods will be gone if they come back later.

'I'll think about it' means 'You have not convinced me that I should have it. Please try again'.

Just go over the attractive points of the item and then SHUT UP. Sometimes you have to do this three times before the punter realizes that they will not leave without the goods OR until they say NO. To a good salesperson, NO means 'sell it to me'. The chance of a sale never ends until the punter walks off.

Mental Attitude

You remember 'Lean-back Jack' earlier on? He won't sell like this. With him, the punter has to beg to buy – it's Jack's way of demeaning people. His pleasure is in feeling superior to the punter because he's scared of them. He has a massive inferiority complex.

A good salesperson knows they are superior to the punter. Equipped with all the little tricks we've learned today, you can 'eat your punters alive'. Jack wouldn't or couldn't learn. That's why he hates the punters – cos most times they win.

You are out there to win. You learn the tricks or go home with Jack's miserable 'take'. You can always blame it on the punters or the weather or the ven... OR on that flash pratt on the next pitch with all the rabbit, who was still taking money when you gave up and went home.

Like I said, 'there's no business like show business'. After a long day of acting the salesman, I go home totally drained but feeling great cos I've got my cash 'Oscar' in the briefcase that's near pulling my left arm out of its socket. It's a sign that the 'audience' enjoyed the 'performance'. Sterling applause if you like.

Chapter 11
The Promoter

When you really know booting and dealing you might consider promoting a sale yourself. I say 'when you really know the game' cos I've seen a lot of folk try to promote and fail. The reason for their failure is usually a lack of knowledge.

The bad booter, who takes poor money, envies the promoter what seems to be easy dough. The theory goes like this.

'I have to find the stock, clean it up, stand in the weather and put up with the punters for a hundred quid or so. And that smart arse (the promoter) gets... well... look (waves arm at ven). Two hundred stalls at five quid a go, that's what?, a grand (£1,000), just to stand and take my money. I'm going to start my own sales!'

I've heard it a thousand times and it is the knell of doom. If you are a poor booter, you will make a poor promoter. You will risk a lot of money and probably lose a lot too. There is more to being a promoter than 'taking pitch money'. Good promoters were good booters first and then moved up when they had the money to risk and the knowledge to succeed.

So how do you become a promoter? I repeat, know the game. Learn what makes a good ven – position, roads, resident population, likely attendance, stewarding, clearing up, security, advertising, food vendors, dealing with trouble makers, observing the laws and the bye-laws. Learn how to be able to deal with authorities, councils, police, site owners, stall holders, the public, loose dogs, lost children, lost property and the press.

Know how to control staff, money, traffic, your temper, the elements (the booters expect you to arrange fine weather). Know what to do when there is a fire, accident, argument, fight, theft, faint, birth (I've seen two souls enter this world at a boot sale), collapse, heart attack, or even death – it happens! (I've seen that too). Where a lot of people gather, 'all human life is there' as they say.

The promoter is the ring-master of the show, and when things go wrong, he's the one expected to crack the whip and put it right. And when it does go right, everyone accuses him of just 'standing and taking money'. Not such a bed of roses, eh?

Now you see why experience and knowledge are the name of the game. Big money equals big responsibility and that 'grand' doesn't stay in the promoter's pocket. A hearty slice goes in overheads – payment for site, advertising, insurance, staff, etc.

And there's still the tax man to be kept happy; and that will mean accountant's bills, book-keeping and the rest. Today's entrepreneur doesn't operate like Arthur Daley. He's in biz the serious way and it's a serious business.

Let's have a chat with Paul, who's been organizing sales for five years and is, in his own modest words, 'fairly successful'.

Paul's Story

I started booting eight years ago. Before that I was a trainee plumber. Some of the stuff we used gave me a bad skin infection and I was advised to leave the trade or my health might suffer. I wanted to go market-trading but just didn't have the dough – so I went booting. I took to it easily and did very well. The outdoors suited me. I liked people and the whole thing.

After three years, I had saved quite a bit of money and was doing a lot of dealing through the week. I was sure that I would be able to keep going without the weekend boot stall and wanted to try organising a sale myself if I could find a venue. It took me a lot of time to find a ven that I would be happy to sell at. There were plenty of places that MIGHT work but I didn't want to use a dog site.

When I found the right place, the owner took a lot of persuading to let me ven it and I had to let him hold a big deposit against things going wrong. He also wanted a weekly fee regardless of weather – but we negotiated a percentage in the end. That took care of the first 20 per cent of the take straight off.

Advertising a new ven takes a lot of dough. And for the first few weeks you make very little because you have to charge low pitch rents to get booters onto an unknown ven. I also had to take out public liability insurance, which seemed a lot then and is terrifying now.

I have five vens on the go at present. I suppose my profit is about 25 per cent of the take – but there's tax to be paid from that and I work something like eighty hours a week. You have to have more than one ven to make it worthwhile. I could make more from booting than I could from one ven.

On Sundays it can be a nightmare. I keep in touch with all the sites by mobile phone and just keep touring round them to deal with problems as they happen. I can often drive as much as two hundred miles during a Sunday to keep everything in order. I have a good site manager at each ven; but good men expect good money.

Although the last ven finishes about 5 p.m., we can still be clearing up at seven – and that's after a 5 a.m. start. Then there's money to be counted and books to be done. It's a rare Sunday I get to bed before 2 or 3 a.m. on Monday, and by that time I've been working and on the go for close to 24 hours. It's not one day a week as people imagine. I take Mondays off. The business keeps me busy the rest of the week.

Vens are never permanent. Two of the current ones will end this year and I have to be on the lookout for replacements. This takes a lot of time and expense in travel, telephones and paperwork.

Promoting is not the casual affair that some people imagine. It's a full-time job with a lot of problems. But I will be honest and say that it's a good living so long as you don't mind work. Sometimes, after a real aggro day, I feel a twinge of envy for the dealers and their free and easy life.

———

Like I said, no bed of roses. Just cos you can work a boot gaff doesn't mean you'll make a promoter. Though he's modest and a very nice guy, Paul is quite a big fish in the promo game and runs a very professional show. You need to be able to take a lot of pressure to get as far as he has.

Fund-Raising Sales

Not all sales are strictly commercial like Paul's. Some are a way for local charities or groups to raise money. These tend to be the smaller affairs and are less organised than the commercial dos. But even so, all the rules and regs have to be observed and the aggros dealt with.

I've met more than one fund-raiser who found boot sales, regardless of the take, to be more than they could handle – particularly if they had full-time employment during the week. You can't work seven days a week for ever. Something's got to give. Most of the fund-raising sales are occasional rather than weekly dos. These offer a lower take to the pro booter, due to the smaller crowds and lower-key advertising.

The bigger one-off charity sales can be very good business. They get heavy press attention because the 'machine' behind a big charry knows all about publicity and goes for 'journalistic' coverage as well as straight advertising. That guarantees a big crowd as long as it don't pissistently (sorry, crude again) pour down with rain.

Big charities know how to organize dos but will bring in a specialist promoter and his staff for a major boot sale. This further underlines how important know-how is in promoting. If it was that easy, the charities would do it themselves.

Weather is of course the big enemy of booter and promoter alike. But here the economic crisis has stepped in to help our slump-driven boom. The glut of empty warehouses and industrial premises has prompted the brighter owner or estate agent to rent out empty buildings on a weekly basis – that is until the economy turns the corner and the sun comes out again.

Warehouse Boot Sales

Pouring rain is just what prompts promoters to hire empty warehouses for boot sales. The indoor sale became the big development of the non-summer of 1992 and continued to flourish through the winter. Promoters, who saw the boot as an outdoor event, lost out to those who rented warehouses and industrial premises for indoor sales.

Indoor sales in halls and such were known before; but what the booter wanted was covered space where the vehicle could be driven in – and large scale warehouses were just that.

The hall-type ven was never big enough for boots. Once the stalls were up, there was no space left for crowds to circulate. If there was, there were too few stalls to attract a good crowd. Whichever way, the take was always poor for both promoter and sellers alike. The warehouse drive-in ven solved the problem of the boot's expansive nature. A whole new range of vens came into being.

I don't need to underline how many empty warehouses and factories are lying idle, just waiting for the chance to become hives of junk-commerce. So, if anyone tells you booting is saturated for want of vens, DON'T YOU BELIEVE IT. Guys like Paul, above, are negotiating rental deals right now and making cash offers that estate agents find hard to refuse.

Do your worst, Mother Nature. We're home and dry. The public will turn out for us as long as they don't have to walk around in the rain. Promoters tell me that covered sales are now drawing larger crowds than open events, with the same number of sellers present. We may have discovered a whole new flock of punters under cover.

Doubling Up

One way of creeping into promoting is 'doubling up'. You find a small site, organize a sale but still run your own stall. Though your take will be lower than at a big sale, you will get pitch money from the other booters – and a small site owner cannot expect vast returns from you for a tiny venue.

Most of your booters will be small timers and two-bobs – but it is a way to learn how it's done without great risk.

You could also consider doing a one-off for a charity or local school. Here the finances are a lot different. If you use, for example, the local school playground and make the school your 'beneficiary' – common practice – the school will expect at least a 50/50 split of the pitch money after the expenses.

Many schools organise their own boot sales as fund-raisers. These are usually held on Saturdays. A Sunday sale at a school is less common since there could be objections from parents, who whilst accepting the need for fund-raising, find Sunday trading unacceptable. This attitude varies widely according to the area. You have to use your knowledge of your part of the world – but it never hurts to ask, does it?

If you double up as booter and promoter/organiser, you will need help. If you are in charge, you can't run your stall and neglect organization. A 'lone wolf' booter can make very good money as a stall holder, but can't run a ven alone. Even if you leave your own stalling-out till everyone is settled down, there will still be latecomers, enquiries, and parking problems – to mention but a few hassles.

You will hardly have time to sell as well as organize. You either have someone to run your stall or have someone to organize under your direction. Either way it must only be seen as a way of gaining experience in organizing, rather than a paying proposition.

It's the old adage: 'the man who wears two hats at the same time finds that neither suit him'. You may feel that promoting is too big a step or that the pleasure of dealing is something you don't want to give up, even for the larger rewards of the full-time promoter.

AGAIN, I emphasize, DON'T attempt promoting before you've been a booter and understand the biz. It's like trying to get in and drive a car on a busy road when you've never been behind the wheel before, and it usually leads to disaster. One or two have succeeded in promoting without being a booter first; but they had experience in other related fields like markets, fairs or outdoor events. It's best to walk before you run.

Other Ways to Expand

By now I may have put you off the idea of promoting. Well I'd rather do that than see you come to grief. Once you get good at booting, promo isn't the only way up. Booters have 'graduated' into other related trades.

There's full market-trading, shops, antique dealing, 'event trading' (that's traders who appear at big outdoor shows, steam fairs, horse trials etc. – usually with a specialist line). For all of these, booting is a good school at which to learn the basics of the business and get paid to do it.

Let's listen to Margaret, who started as a booter and now has a specialist shop.

Margaret's Story

My husband Roy died from a heart attack seven years ago and I thought it was the end of the world. Fortunately the children were all but grown up and Roy's insurances took care of immediate money worries.

But money doesn't go far today and, within a year, I realised that I would have to go back to work to have anything like a reasonable life. The thought of starting again (I hadn't worked since we started a family eighteen years ago) terrified me. I had no real skills and there were a lot of people looking for jobs.

I must admit it was the kids that got me going. We were clearing out the shed and garage, about eighteen months after Roy went, when my son talked me into doing a boot sale. I didn't like the idea at first but, as the kids said, I needed to get out into the world again. Roy's death had hit me very hard.

That first time was an eye-opener. I had never even been to a boot sale and was staggered when we – the kids and my sister all helped – came home with over £200! For the first time in ages, I enjoyed myself.

Before my marriage I had worked in one of the old-fashioned haberdashers shops that have all but gone now. It was nothing like booting, all very Victorian and prim, but I did pick up some knowledge of linen and lace in the two years I was there.

It started to come back to me as I looked around boot stalls that first time. I bought a lovely set of Edwardian antimacassars for 50p, laid them out on our stall and got £6 for them! It just went on from there. At first, when all the stuff from home was gone, I spent time going round boots and jumble sales to find things to sell. I did a sale about every three weeks.

I put an advert in the paper asking for 'granny's bottom drawer stuff' and got a lot of replies. By the end of a year, I was a 'specialist' concentrating on linen, lace, old jewellery and fans. It was a growing field of collecting. People frame that sort of thing to display, like pictures.

For the past two years I have run my own shop in an antiques centre. Though I liked the boot sale atmosphere, the weather can be tiresome at my age and my stock needs the right kind of permanent display and lighting.

I get customers from all over the world, tourists and collectors, and I still go to boots to find stock. It's incredible really that a pair of Edwardian bloomers, sold for the 'disgraceful price' of two shillings (ten pence, today) ninety years ago, can now fetch thirty to forty pounds! – or even more if they have the fine silk embroidery of the moneyed classes.

I am now a 'business lady'. I never dreamed that I would own, well rent, a shop, and I laugh at how scared I was at the thought of going out to work again.

I have a nice sideline in framing collectables as gifts, and also in pictures from the Victorian and Edwardian eras – mostly fashion plates and the like. Costume is a big market. I have just had a dress sold at auction for

£400; and I intend to take on another shop unit to display collectable costume in the same building as my current shop.

———

There you go. Another boot success story. Age or sex matters not a jot – just the ability to get up and go. Specializing is another way for the booter looking to expand. But it's that basic training in booting that teaches you what's what. How to buy and sell, how to deal with the public and, most important of all, how not to WASTE money.

This is something many shopkeepers never learn – and that's why so many shops go bust. They just haven't got the survival techniques that become second nature to the booter. It's one of the reasons why so many Asian folk make good shopkeepers. They learnt their trade in basic market-trading and applied those methods to shopkeeping.

Margaret makes a lot of money from her biz. Her prices frighten the hell out of me. But on Saturdays in particular you can't move in her shop – it's so crowded.

I always take costume, old linen etc. to Margaret. She pays cash on the nail and knows how to do a deal. She also knows the stuff inside out and can identify things that mystify me. Museum people deal with her and I think she's toying with the idea of writing a book – though how she'll find the time with two shops to run, Lord only knows. But that's the nature of dealers. They'll find time if it pays.

Chapter 12
What do I do with All this Dough?

Money is the root of all evil, they say. Actually it's poverty that is at the root of evil and the effort to escape its clutches can lead to some evil doings.

But what if you find yourself, after years of scratching around, with what is known as an embarrassment of riches? Many folk who take a quick jump up the financial ladder soon realize that there are as many problems in having a fair bit of dosh as there are in having none at all.

Football pool winners are a good example; but they get advice and guidance from the nice chaps sent along by the Pools company to see they don't get themselves in a mess. Even so, quite a few do – probably because they didn't take the nice man's advice and thought they could handle the odd few hundred thou and no problem.

Now I'm not saying that you are going to have that kind of dough under the bed five minutes after starting booting. But it's surprising how easy it is to get carried away when you find the old weekly pittance has become a few hundred. Careful management is required to avoid trouble and it's better to start sooner than later.

So lets take a look at the cash problems that can loom up for the new booter.

Early Days

Many booters, as we have seen earlier, got into the game out of sheer desperation. The relief of having some real cash in their hands is often soon overshadowed by worries. What if they are still receiving state benefits? What about the tax man?

Sometimes they suffer from an uneasy feeling that it just can't be right to be able to earn this kind of cash so easily. These are all very natural reactions. Let's take them one at a time.

State Benefits

Back in the depression of the 1930s, the 'Means Test' was a nightmare for the poor who were forced on to state benefit, or Unemployment Relief as it was called. The few crumbs of comfort offered by the Poor Law Guardians of each parish were given grudgingly; and the expression 'cold as charity' is a lenient description of the worthy burghers who decided the qualifications for a hand-out.

In those days of massive unemployment poor people had precious little. To receive benefit, they were forced by the Inspector to sell everything of value in their home and to use the proceeds to survive, before they could be termed 'truly needy'.

Some folk say that we are fast approaching the same situation again. But today's smart claimants are one step ahead. All excess-to-requirement goods are 'down the booter', regardless of the (today, non-existent) Inspector. The proceeds of such operations should not be regarded as income for the purposes of calculating State Benefit entitlement. You can sell your OWN goods quite legally without generating income.

You must however draw the line between what was YOURS and what you obtained TO SELL. You can argue that it is a grey area as wide as the Atlantic – but the principle is clear.

If you get hold of a radio and listen to it for five minutes, it could be construed that it was your property (for however short a time) which you used and had the benefit of and THEN decided to sell – in which case, still NOT income.

That argument may impress you but it is most unlikely to impress an Inspector. He would probably argue that buying something in order to sell it for profit is evidence of trading. And any proceeds from that trade IS income.

Captial Gains Tax

There is also the question of Capital Gains Tax – but there's even more grey water clouding that. Broadly, this tax is payable when you sell something of yours for more money than you paid for it.

At present, you can make £5,800 profit during the year (after taking off the cost price) on the sale of your own goods before you need to worry about Capital Gains Tax. This amount is usually increased by the Chancellor in each Budget, and the 'cost price' of your goods may also be increased in line with inflation.

That's about £111 a week PLUS ORIGINAL COST taken care of for a start. With 'creative accounting' it could cover you for rather more.

When you add it up, it's amazing the amount of money you and all your relatives wasted over the last ten years on things you never needed at all – isn't it?

Income Support

This is a Social Security benefit to help people whose income is below a certain level and who are not working for 16 hours a week or more. You'll know if you're on it.

The big factor here is savings. The benefit is affected by savings of more than £3,000 and is currently not payable at all if you and your partner have £8,000 in the bank or wherever.

Moral? Perhaps you shouldn't put your booting proceeds in the bank, but use them as business capital. What is or is not 'savings' could take years to argue out – by which time you would have retired to your villa in the South of France and would long since have stopped drawing benefits cos you couldn't find the time to 'sign on' anyway. This is a complex subject and you really must take proper advice. Don't take risks. Ask first.

I'm being a little facetious here, because any one who goes booting seriously will quickly dispense with the State's help once they see the returns for their efforts.

One or two creeps cheat and claim benefits when they are earning the kind of money that makes the working man's take-home look like pocket money. When they do get caught by investigators, puzzled as to why a bloke on the dole has a brand new Mercedes outside his house, they've only themselves to blame. Don't you agree?

The Sunday Secret

A lot of decent folk coming into booting worry that they might be making themselves 'unavailable for work' by booting if they are claiming 'The Feed All' or 'Bun' (Unemployment Benefit). 'Why don't investigators from the dole check on boot sales?', is a question often asked by new booters.

The answer may be 'six days shalt thou be available for work'. What you do on Sunday, whether that be to worship Maker or Mammon, is your own biz. God's wrath shall descend on any dole official insisting on availability on Sundays. And no doubt also the wrath of Her Gracious Majesty the Queen, God bless her, as Defender of the Faith.

Persons visiting boot sales should be aware of the dangers of carrying a black briefcase. Such action can be injurious to the health, or at least to personal dignity. Objects falling at random from the sky are attracted to such cases. The carrier can also get a strange sensation of becoming invisible, inaudible or even of developing a strange foreign tongue that no one can understand. It can be very upsetting and can spoil a nice Sunday.

Enterprise Allowance

This government scheme means basically: 'start your own biz whilst claiming allowances'.

The idea is that, for a year, you are paid £40 a week to start your own show. Snag is you have to come up with £1, 000 of your own cash to 'pass go'. Some folk on this scheme have gone straight into market trading.

I tried to get figures regarding the success or otherwise of market trader type ventures under the scheme from a Local Enterprise Agency and was told that they are unable 'at present' to provide statistics regarding individual types of trade.

The spokesperson also remarked that 'certain types of trade' might not be acceptable to the scheme.

What does that all mean? You're as wise as I am. If you have a 'grand' spare and are claiming U.B., try an application. Like I've said before, it never hurts to ask.

If you're the type I think you are, and have a 'grand' doing nothing, you probably don't need the government's help to get your dough working now you've got this book.

Tax Man

He is not the villain he is painted – as long as you have a hero to protect you. Heroes in this drama come in the form of accountants. If you start a new biz or find that a 'hobby' is starting to pay off, a short interview with an accountant is common sense.

I can never understand some folks' fear of the tax man. You don't pay tax unless you earn money. If you do, there are miles of allowances to set against your earnings before you pay tax. If you earn lots of money, you can pay your tax and no worries. The accountant will see that you pay no more than you have to.

Most fear is born of ignorance. The tax man will not be hammering on your door the minute you make your first fiver. In fact he's not all that interested in the first £2,500! If you start a new biz, he's quite content to wait over a year before asking if there's anything in it for him. And then he's not too surprised if his cut is less than enough to keep one light bulb burning in his office till the end of next year.

Despite all you may hear to the contrary, the allowances for a new biz are very attractive. Businesses fail due to crippling overheads, bad debts, lack of customers and interest on loans. None of these problems are the concern of the booter/dealer. They should never happen to you. Your money will not be eaten up by them; and tax should never be a problem.

Accountant

Always choose a qualified CHARTERED ACCOUNTANT. Your first thirty-minute interview should cost NOTHING and you will learn much to your advantage.

There are those who call themselves accountants and have few or no qualifications. They usually ask for money for an interview.

You can do your own books if you wish, but an accountant should save you far more than his fees in tax AVOIDANCE – that's legal. Tax EVASION is illegal and can also earn you free accommodation from the prison service!

V.A.T.

This should be discussed with your accountant. You have to be taking over £700 a week before it NEED concern you – and that's with overheads of near nothing.

Investments

Again, you talk to the accountant. There are many ways of making money work for you and minimising tax. But there are ways that are a little strange, even to financial experts. The antique dealer's system is interesting.

The 'Home Furnishing' Investment Scheme

In this scheme, the dealer starts with an empty house. He buys very astutely and furnishes the house tastefully with his purchases. The house becomes not only his living accommodation but also a sort of showroom for the 'stock' – which is his personal furniture.

When the market is right, a piece is sent for sale at a substantial profit, or it may be sold to a 'visitor'. Stuff always looks better in a 'home' setting. Sales are of course replaced by new purchases.

The benefits are enormous – no storage costs and a free showroom. There are a host of other advantages. This scheme is run in conjunction with a proper business, naturally. It's a bit like having a free car and no service or repair bills because you own the garage.

The tax aspect needs careful watching. If you are 'trading', tax will have to be paid on the profits. Even if what you are disposing of can genuinely be classed as your own goods, a liability may be incurred in the form of Capital Gains Tax.

The antique dealer's money is safely 'invested' in the goods around him or her. There are also savings on furniture for the home. Booters can operate a similar scheme with modern stuff.

I know of one guy who even re-packages his disposable razors and sells them. Now there's a novelty. He hasn't put out a dustbin in years! If you are real smart, every purchase becomes an investment. There's nothing that can't be re-sold.

It's cash that counts. If you're going to invest, the one requirement is the money to do it. Let's have a chat with 'French Terry', whose cash operations have made him an international dealer on a small but very profitable scale.

Terry's Tale

I was a clerk in a large insurance office. The money was so poor that I started doing boot sales at weekends, just to keep my car on the road and make ends meet. I got my stuff by going around skips and what-not in the evenings.

It wasn't long before I went booting full-time. I earned more than my week's wages at the office in four hours on a Sunday morning. I had a brilliant day one Sunday and just didn't bother to turn up for work any more. It took a month for them to realize I wasn't there!

I had a very steady girlfriend and we used to enjoy the boots, working together on the stall. It was fun. The big thing happened for me when we went on a weekend package trip to Paris.

I wanted to go to the 'Flea Market' that you see in films and on T.V.; and Di, my girl, wanted to see the fashion places an' that.

We had a great time, but what got me was the prices the French guys were getting for their stuff at the Flea. These were ten times more than a good boot price – particularly for cigarette lighters, watches (the old sort, not class) and just 50's run-of-the-mill gear. Old British suits, like 40's and 50's heavy-weight stuff was fetching fortunes!

Now the only French I knew was school stuff. (I did go to a grammar school and hated it.) A lot of the French 'booters' spoke English and we got chatting to a couple – they get a lot of tourists at the Flea and English is a sort of common language. We told them about Brit booting and they were quite interested. We got really friendly with this French bloke, Marc, who was about our age. He said he would buy all the Brit suits I could find, if I could get them over to him.

That was it! Over the next three months, I raided every charry, jumbly or whatever for old suits. I also started buying in lighters, watches an' stuff.

We booked a ferry crossing and drove all the way to Paris. It was right hairy that first time and I thought we'd never make it. All the way, I kept having nightmares that it would go wrong and I would be stuck with the old tat. But when we got to the Flea, we found Marc and he reckoned the gear as knockout (very good).

To keep it brief, I made a profit of £270 on the whistles (suits). I'd paid like a pound and one-fifty each for them in Brit. Marc paid the French equivalent of 15 to 18 quid EACH! He also took me to see a guy who made my day by paying close to £500 for a briefcase full of lighters and stuff. The whole lot cost me about £40!

That first trip showed a profit of just under £500 after travel and what-not. I changed the French dough into English before we came back. You get a better exchange rate like that.

Today, I make the Paris trip once a month. I then move up to Belgium, where I buy oriental rugs with the French dough. The rugs are dirt cheap there, I can get ten times the price in Brit. I aim to convert the Brit tot into French dough at a profit of 1,000 per cent, then spend it on rugs in Belg at a further 1,000 per cent profit back in Brit.

£100 spent on tot becomes £10,000 in three days! That's plus buying-time in Brit. I'm getting into class ant in Brit now – gotta do something with the dough!

A round trip costs me about £400 in exes. And do you know, not once have the Customs said a word about what I'm carrying. It looks so little really. Now with the new regs, they don't even look in the motor – except the occasional check for drugs and stuff, and that's not my thing at all.

Oh yeah, I've got quite chatty in 'Fronglais' as it's called, and me an' Di got married last autumn. The honeymoon? Paris of course. Vive La France! I say.

———

What a smart boy, eh? And you thought £500 a week was stretching it!

There's more. Lads like Terry are spreading out right across Europe. There are big spoils to be had in countries like Poland, Russia and Bulgaria. The borders are down. Cash rules.

Just last week, I met a guy importing 'champagne' from Russia at £3 a case (10 bottles). It sells for £7.50 A BOTTLE in London. All you need is cash and courage. It's a bit beyond car boot sales; but all these people started by doing little deals that taught them their business.

Dealing and money are international. Biz is biz wherever you are. You just have to keep your eyes open, your wits about you, and know your trade. The cash comes from work and the courage comes from confidence in your ability. It's the old saying 'earn the pennies and the pounds follow'.

Chapter 13
The Way Ahead

Can It Continue?

I was working a sale last August bank holiday. The weather hadn't been all that bright but the punters, bless 'em, turned out like good 'uns.

Pitched beside me was an old mate Colin and his wife Stella. They were doing a roaring trade in ghastly wall-mounted telephones – horrid colours but all new and boxed at £6 each.

Coll and I went 'walkabout' (I had help on the gaff) to see if there was anything worth having on other stalls. We 'stole' a few odds and ends from the two-bobs and amateurs and then went for a cuppa before going back.

Coll was telling me about his week-end. 'I've been out (selling) all four days this holiday – Friday evening, Saturday, Sunday and today' he said. 'Given I had good stuff, I've took close to a grand up to now'.

'You're not complaining, I hope, Coll', I said, teasing a bit.

'No, mate no, but you can't help thinking it can't go on, can you?'

Sometimes it seems like that to me. It seems impossible that you can keep on turning rubbish into money at that rate – that one day, the rubbish will run out or the punters will get fed up and not come anymore.

I thought back to when I began booting and I started to laugh. 'What's the joke?' says Coll. 'Well', says I, 'the first sale I ever did, there was a bloke pitched next door and he kept saying the same thing. Every time he put a note in his pocket, he said 'this can't go on, it's not possible'. And that was back when pound notes were still around, Coll.

Coll burst out laughing too; and we stood there splitting ourselves like a couple of pratts until an old girl remarked that it was disgusting to see men drunk at a family do!

The boot thing just goes on getting bigger and bigger. Sure, there must come an end one day. Nothing lasts for ever. But that day's not next week or next year.

It's somewhere in the distant future, when everyone can have everything they want at a price they can afford. Utopia is as far away now as it was a hundred years ago when the early socialists first dreamed of it. It will probably never come and, if it does, life will be downright boring.

It's the little adventures that make life fun. Someone once said: 'Marriage is the one adventure open to cowards'. A boot sale is somewhat similar. It is a little adventure – a walk with minimum risk on the slightly unruly side, full of small surprises.

The Changing Scene

Things will change of course. Today's boot sale is a far more sophisticated affair than it was twenty years ago. And it will go on developing itself and also go on giving folk the opportunity to develop themselves by starting in biz for nothing and with no risk.

As new faces come in, others use the capital they made from booting to move on to more conventional businesses.

People retire from booting, just as they do from any other form of trade. Booters become promoters, market traders, shopkeepers and whatever.

Dealers say: 'You never retire'. There is some truth in this for once you get dealing in your blood, it's hard to shake off. Many of the old timers who come to sales are 'retired' dealers who give you a hell of a run for your money once the haggling starts.

They will tell stories of outrageous rip-offs back in the horse-and-cart days and can be a mine of information. Talking to them, you soon realise that there's not much new under the sun. You can learn a lot from these veterans of the game, as I did.

'Green Boots'

Some developments are non-starters. I well remember a venue opened by a well-meaning group that was an absolute disaster. They advertised what they called a 'friendly' sale and it wasn't till their booters turned up on the day that its 'friendly' nature was revealed.

First they wanted the names, addresses, phone numbers and car registrations of all sellers. They had their own stall on site and didn't charge pitch money – just a nominal 50p. But they wanted all sellers to leave a £5 deposit 'in case of disputes with buyers'.

None of that went down too well – nor did the card with a large number that you had to display by your flash so that the punter could identify you. As if that wasn't enough, they wanted to check all stock as it went on display. It was 'we can't allow this', 'we don't allow that'.

Of course a nasty scene developed and most of the boots left. Those who stuck it, 'dogged out' (took nothing); and the punters didn't stay for five minutes. 'There's nothing to buy' was their universal comment.

What was it all in aid of? Search me! A colleague reckoned it was the brain child of some 'green type' who had paid 10p for a clockwork mouse at a boot and found that its spring was broken. It was a personal crusade to clean up the boot game.

Cleaner Booting

The punters don't want clean booting. Half the fun is taking a chance – a sort of gamble with low stakes. When they've bought enough useless old tot, they start booting themselves.

The only thing that can threaten booting is legislation to bring it into line with High Street shops. Such legislation is virtually beyond framing – for politicians are well aware that the public likes boot sales. They might as well try to increase their popularity by banning football or closing down the pubs.

The raffish side of the boot is a part of its attraction. Clean it up and you spoil it. You might as well stop all sport because people get hurt. The public knows full well that people take a chance when they buy boot gear. For the massive amount of stuff sold, there are very few complaints – less in fact than in many supposedly 'straighter' operations.

If boot sales are as great an evil as some minor politicos or cranky writers of letters-to-the-editor would like us to believe, the public would long since have deserted us and there would be no sales.

You have only to study the figures at the start of this book to see that the public judges for itself. It wants boot sales as a form of entertainment and fun. As one lady punter said to me: 'It's a bit like a fairground – you know you might get caught but at least you get a prize every time you pay out some money'.

For those folk who imagine they will get the same quality at a boot as in a High-Street shop, there should perhaps be a sign that says 'Caveat Emptor' or 'You get what you pay for'. But would they read or take heed of it? I doubt it. The saying 'there's one born every minute' is a serious underestimate.

Prices in the Shops

Others see the boot as a regular provider of what they can't afford in the shops – odds and ends that are simply beyond their budget at new (retail) prices. I, along with most other booters, find shop prices appallingly high and rarely buy there.

It's not altogether the shopkeepers' fault. Rents and business rates have become ridiculous. I know I'm being a bit political here, but it has to be said that greedy landlords and wastrel Local Authorities are as much to blame as anyone for the economic mess our country's in.

Landlords – not in the sense of the individual property owner but large consortiums – care nothing for providing genuine shopping facilities. They create developments for investment which destroy the cheaper shops. They then bleed their tenants dry with ever-increasing rents until they go bust. You only have to look at the number of empty units in shopping malls to see what a crumbling house of cards the whole thing has become.

There are still shoppers in the malls – but not as many as there were in the High Streets a few years back. If you want to see shopping crowds today, go to a boot sale. I wonder how many enemies of boot sales have money invested in shopping malls – and how many of the hostile 'Letters to the Editor' are phoneys aimed at shutting down a dangerous competitor?

A People's Market

We in the biz have often thought the boot might develop into a kind of peoples' market, where folk can obtain goods at prices that are not inflated by extortionate overheads. This is already happening in some places where the recession is deepest. There, boots are moving away from just junk and are starting to supply the whole range of household goods at affordable prices.

The shops don't like this; and we are going to see more artful and spidery attempts to stop boots and force folk to pay higher prices. These moves will be made under the cloak of safety and crime prevention. Oh what tangled webs these artful spiders weave – and they call booters crooks!

Your Future

But what of your own future?

I have tried to tell you how to start and have also passed on a few wrinkles. Some of those described are slightly offensive, some are funny and – I hope you will agree – many are fascinating. Your future is in your own hands. So is your decision to give it a go. But I do promise that you can't lose out by trying it.

I would like, on your behalf and mine, to thank all the folk who gave their time and revealed not a few secrets so that you can know what really goes on in the ducking-and-diving world. As you will have read, nearly all of them started with damn all and have become successful – some severely so, as we say in the biz. I didn't have to scour the country to find them. There are hundreds more like them, possibly thousands – and there's room for lots more.

Someone's got to get this country moving and it might just be us. O.K., so it's a junk economy – but it's a healthy one and full of smart money.

A bankrupt booter is as rare as rocker's droppings (I'll leave you to work that one out) – though some bankrupts have booted their way out of bankruptcy! It's a kind trade and it rejects no one. All are welcome as long as they play the game.

I will chance my arm a little bit and venture to say that this book is probably the best buy you have ever made. Not only will following what I've told you get your dough back in a week, it could easily make you as wealthy as some of the folk you've read about. You may even do better.

It's up to you now. You can put this book on a shelf and say the author's full of bull – or you can go out and prove that he isn't. There are the two choices. I hope you'll prove me right; cos if you go for it, you'll find it near impossible to prove me wrong.

I've said it before and I'll say it again. If you go to a boot sale and dump junk in front of the punters you can't fail to make money. Do it right and you'll make good money. Become a full-time dealer and you will get rich. And I hope you do!

Right! Off you go then. Get that shed cleared out and I'll see you down the ven, nice and early. An' if you see me first, it's two sugars in mine and I like me bacon crispy.

Be LUCKY. And remember, the harder you try the luckier you get. All the best!

Glossary

Some of the 'dealer' terms most frequently used in the text:

Ant	antique
Booter	a car boot seller
Charries	charity shops
Civilians	non-dealers
Coll, collectables	items of value only to collectors
Dogs	dud goods
Flash	the frontage of a stall
Front line	in front of a stall
A Grand	£1,000
Gaff	the selling area of a stall
A Jacks	£5
Job	a big lot sold cheaply
Manor	home area
Mark-up	profit
A Monkey	£500
A Oner	£100
Pot	china items
Punter	a customer
Recce	reconnaissance
Schmo	an easily led punter
Shadow	a crook who fakes dogs to look like first class goods
Spiel	sales talk
Stalling out	setting up the stall
Tip	Local Authority rubbish dump
Tom	jewellery
Tot	goods retrieved for gain e.g. from dustbins
Two-bob	small-time, of no account financially or socially
Trader	market stall-holder
Ven	site of car boot sale

Dealer slang is a mixture of cockney rhyming slang, Gypsy, Yiddish and back slang. It also contains many terms from the racetrack.